P9-DGL-480

NOT JUST VERY FAST. BUT VERY GOOD.

There's a catch to using this book.

The Clean Team has timed and tested every sequence, technique, and product. They know what works. They tell you what to do. And they are The Boss.

They teach you a simple system for the whole house. They give you diagrams that help. They lead you step-by-step. They threaten you if you do it wrong!

The result is a sparkling clean home in under half the time you used to take. Very clean. Very fast. Very easy.

What's the catch? You do it their way. No arguments. No discussions. No compromises.

Why? Because it works!

SPEED CLEANING

FOR THOSE WHO WOULD RATHER BE DOING PRACTICALLY ANYTHING ELSE.

SPEED CLEANING

Jeff Campbell
and
The Clean Team

A DELL TRADE PAPERBACK

Published by
Dell Publishing
a division of
The Bantam Doubleday Dell Publishing Group, Inc.
666 Fifth Avenue
New York, New York 10103
A first edition of this book was self-published by the author.

Copyright © 1985, 1987 by Jeff Campbell
Illustrations copyright © 1987 by Axelle Foriter, SF, CA.

All rights reserved. No part of this book may be repro-
duced or transmitted in any form or by any means,
electronic or mechanical, including photocopying, re-
cording or by any information storage and retrieval system, without the written permission of the Publisher, except where permitted by law.
The trademark Dell® is registered in the U.S. Patent and
Trademark Office.

ISBN: 0-440-58015-3

Printed in the United States of America

April 1987

10 9 8

S

Acknowledgments

Bill Redican, Ph.D., editor and friend, contributed much of what is good, clever, and fun in this effort. He helped write and rewrite this whole project. Thank you.

Special thanks to Keith Taylor, who trusts me for some reason or another and fights with me only when I'm wrong or when he's in the mood.

George Johnston sacrificed vacation time to type several chapters, which is a favor I wouldn't have done even for myself.

Dedication

To my friends and partners at The Clean Team. Before them I mistakenly thought that work wasn't any fun. Thanks to them I look forward to weekdays also.

And, to our very special clients and friends who invested the real money that allowed the freedom to complete this book.

Table of Contents

INTRODUCTION

Naturally, cleaning house may not be your favorite pastime. You can *hate* it as far as we're concerned. Whatever your attitude toward housecleaning, we can teach you how to get it over with in half the time or less. Guaranteed.

Our grandmothers were able to devote their full time to keeping house. But these days most of us are left wondering where all our time went—with working, commuting, raising a family, entertaining, and all those other demands on our time. The dirt didn't go away, but leisure time did, and with less leisure time there is a lot less time for things like cleaning.

Wouldn't you love to have some extra time for a change? We assume that you would rather be doing practically anything else with your precious leisure time than cleaning your house or apartment. So this book is just as much about personal freedom as it is about cleaning.

Most time-consuming activities have been analyzed, studied, and boiled down to the fastest, smartest methods possible. These activities have evolved an economy and precision of movement that have yet to be applied to the task that consumes more of your leisure time than any other: cleaning house.

This is the first such treatment for housecleaning. It's going to give you back your weekends.

Ours is a hardheaded, streamlined, step-by-step approach. We're not offering you a collection of household hints (and there are lots of them in books and newspapers). All the hints rolled up together with a ribbon around them won't tell you *how to clean the house*. Household hints may tell you how to make a sponge smell sweet again. We say, "Who cares?! Throw it away!" Our method is for people who want to get cleaning over with and move on to better things—not fuss, discuss, or otherwise linger over it. It's astonishing that housecleaning can be reduced to such a short period of time.

This book is also intended for families who are redistributing household duties less strictly according to gender and more evenly throughout the household. (We're talking about husbands who are always in trouble for not doing their share around the house.) To husbands who may have a lack of skill or interest in housecleaning, this book will offer a linear, hands-on approach that is more appealing than traditional methods. Besides, learning to clean a bathroom in 12 minutes may be a relatively small price to pay for the harmony it will add to a marriage or relationship.

This is a system of weekly cleaning: bathroom, kitchen, dusting, and vacuuming. No, we're not going to tell you how to put dirty clothes in the hamper or the children's toys away. That's a daily job. (We do give you some encouragement in Chapter 10, however.) But take heart. We've seen over and over again that those problems start taking care of themselves as a sense of pride in a clean home encourages everyone in the family to keep the house civilized between weekly cleanings.

This method was developed by The Clean Team—San Francisco's pre-eminent housecleaning service. For over six years we've kept records of every visit to thousands of households in San Francisco. We've timed and tested every sequence, technique, and product imaginable. The result was no accident, and this method enables our teams to clean without a wasted motion—not by working harder, just smarter. And besides being fast, we're very, very good: Our waiting list has often been six months long.

Two things before we start. First, we work in teams of three. If there's just one of you, that's even more efficient: You'll just do each job in sequence. Two works well also. If there are four of you, rotate one person "off" each time you clean.

Second, we're the boss. Maybe you'll develop your own method some-day, but for now we're going to relieve you of the burden of making decisions. No arguments. No discussions. No compromises. *We're the boss.* We can clean three or four times faster than you . . . and better. We have to. We clean San Francisco homes 10,000 times a year. And our three-person teams can clean an average house in 42 minutes—start to finish. A one-bedroom apartment takes about 21 minutes!

Believe your eyes! We didn't say *"Saturday afternoon."* We said "42 minutes" because we're as good as they come. We used time-and-motion analysis and an endless comparison of cleaning products and equipment to develop a method that would save every step and every moment possible. And now we're going to teach *you.*

THE CLEAN TEAM RULES

Here are our trade secrets. We observe every one of them. Every day.

1. **Make every move count.** That means work around the room once. Don't backtrack. It also means you must carry your equipment and supplies with you so you don't make dozens of aggravating trips back and forth across the room. Walk around the room once and you're done, except for the floor.

2. **Use the right tools.** Ah! Here's probably the major timesaver of the bunch. Give your specialized gadgets to your enemies. You need real tools that cut time to shreds. Most of all, you need a *work apron* to hang tools on and store cleaning supplies in as you move around the room. The method depends on it and soon you'll feel lost without yours. If you don't have one, we'll tell you how to get one later in the book (p. 16).

3. **Work from top to bottom.** Always. Period. Don't argue.

4. **If it isn't dirty, don't clean it.** For example, vertical surfaces are almost never as dirty as horizontal surfaces. Upper shelves have less dust than lower ones. The same with upper and lower molding.

5. **Don't rinse or wipe a surface before it's clean.** You'll just have to start over. In other words, when you're cleaning a surface, don't rinse or wipe just to see if you're done. If you were wrong, you'll have to start all over again. Learn to check as you're cleaning by "seeing through" the gunk to the surface below. Then you can tell when it's dislodged and ready to be wiped or rinsed . . . *once!*

6. **Don't keep working after it's clean.** Once you've reached ground zero, *stop!* You're cutting into VLT—Valuable Leisure Time. Rinse or wipe and move on.

7. **If what you're doing isn't going to work, then shift to a heavier-duty cleaner or tool.** You're going to get very good at knowing what tool or product to use without having to throw everything in the book at it. You'll be learning to anticipate what to reach for *before* you start a task so you won't have to shift.

8. **Keep your tools in impeccable shape.** Dull razors scratch—they don't clean. Clogged spray bottles puff up and make funny noises—they don't spray.

9. Repetition makes for smoother moves. Always put your tools back in the same spot in your apron. You can't spare the time to fumble around for them. And you can't afford to leave them lying around in alien places for the dog to carry away. You'll quickly get so expert you'll become aggravated if the tool you expected isn't in the right spot when you reach for it. Progress, progress.

10. Pay attention. Almost everything else will fall into place if you do. Don't think about the revisions in the tax code. Or anything else. In Latin: *Age quod agis*—"Do what you are doing."

11. Keep track of your time. Get a little faster every time.

12. Use both hands. Your work force is half idle if one hand is doing all the work. Finish one step with one hand and start the next step with the other. Or, wipe with one hand while the other steadies the object.

13. If there are more than one of you, work as a team. You're what the biologists call a "superorganism." If your partner gets done 10 minutes faster, the *team* gets done 10 minutes faster. And that is a wonderful thing. You cannot stop being vigilant for one moment about what will speed up or slow down your partner's progress.

That's it. Like any new skill, Speed Cleaning must be learned, practiced, reviewed, and perfected. It's worth it. The payoff is that you will save hours every week. Hours that add up to days that you will now spend *not* cleaning the house.

These are the basics. The rest of the book consists of specialized sections on tools, products, and jobs. Read the following chapter on tools and products. After that, if you're going to clean the kitchen, you are the "Kitchen Person," and so you should read the Kitchen Manual next. The "Bathroom Person" and "Duster" should read the Bathroom Manual and Duster Manual respectively. If you are working alone, read the Kitchen Manual after Chapter 2 and take a break before reading on.

TOOLS AND PRODUCTS

There are tools needed to do the job of cleaning that are indispensable. If you don't have them, you're going to have to get them—that's all there is to it—even though you may have been getting along without some of them for years.

After you're equipped with the proper tools, guard against the entire Speed Cleaning process being slowly sabotaged because of tools wearing out or supplies running low. Replace as necessary. We're offering you time to spend *not* cleaning. Get and keep supplies and tools.

The strict rules you have learned about cleaning also apply to storing your cleaning supplies. Your tools are too important for you to have them scattered around the house where they could be lost, damaged, or not available when they are needed. If you are going to clean your house in 42 minutes, you can't spend 22 minutes gathering your supplies. We'll tell you where each item is stored and who uses it in the Kitchen, Bathroom, and Duster Manuals.

Remember we're talking about speed, and the products we recommend offer speed while maintaining high quality. We appreciate the fact that there are premium products that we don't mention (e.g., paste waxes), but our job is to teach you speed. These are the products we use. (Be sure to follow manufacturer's instructions.)

Work apron. Nothing makes sense in this system without the work apron. It saves more time than all the other products combined. It carries the supplies and tools that allow you to "walk around the room once and you're done" (see Rule 1). If you're mad at having to wear one, especially with all this stuff packed into it and dangling off it, go ahead and have your tantrum. Then get over it. *Wear it when cleaning—start to finish.*

The Clean Team uses our own special aprons (see p. 16) featured in the illustrations of this book. You can make your own apron, too, or modify an apron that you have bought in a hardware store or from a catalog. It won't be *exactly* the same as The Clean Team's aprons, but just be sure it has lots of pockets for your tools, loops for your red and blue juice, and will tie securely around your waist. Wear it every time you clean!

A smart way to tie the apron on is to put it on backward, tie it, and turn it around. The Clean Team apron has seven pockets, three of which are dedicated to the following tools:

Toothbrush.

Razor-blade holder.

Scraper.

A fourth pocket is used as a temporary storage for debris you encounter

while cleaning. This saves extra trips to the trash. Use a gallon-size Ziploc storage bag as a liner and paper clips (as shown) to keep it in place.

Carryall tray. Permanent storage for cleaning supplies.

Red juice (in a spray bottle). Heavy-duty liquid cleaner. Professional cleaners call it "red juice" because the commercial concentrate often is red. Retail products include 409, Fantastik, and similar spray-on liquid cleaners. For simplicity's sake, we're going to call it "red juice" in this book. Use it for spray-and-wipe jobs except mirrors and window glass.

Blue juice (in a spray bottle). Light-duty liquid cleaner. Similarly, most professional light-duty liquid cleaners happen to be blue. Consumer products include Windex or any similar liquid cleaner. Use it to spray and wipe mirrors and window glass.

Bleach (in a spray bottle). Use it to remove mold and mildew in the bathroom. Clorox has a relatively new version of bleach (Fresh Scent) that has a far less disagreeable odor than standard bleach.

Spray bottles (three of them). Use them for red juice, blue juice, and bleach. Our model has a handle that fits well on the apron loops. Adjust the spray by turning the nozzle. If it won't spray easily, clean the end of the tube inside the bottle with your toothbrush, or force water through it backward.

Tile juice (in a squirt bottle). Use it to clean soap scum and mineral buildup from the tub/shower area. A variety of liquid tile cleaners is on the market, like Tilex or Lime-A-Way.

Squirt bottle. Use it to apply tile juice. Any tile cleaner you purchase should already be in a container like this. If not, transfer it. An old shampoo bottle works well.

Feather duster. We are well aware of the purists who insist that feather dusters only move the dust around and don't get rid of it. We agree wholeheartedly that dust does need to be controlled in the home as much as possible. In some cases, this can mean wiping the dust up with furniture polish and a cloth, or washing baseboards, or vacuuming shelves. However, when maintaining a basically clean home on a regular basis, moving a small amount of dust very quickly from one (higher) level to another (lower) level where most of it is vacuumed away is a decidedly good thing. And a good feather duster happens to do this better than anything else. Get an air purifier if you are kept awake at night wondering what happened to all the dust.

The only feather duster that works is made with real feathers—ostrich down to be exact. Down feathers are full, soft, and almost spiderweb-like at the ends. The feather duster we use is 18 inches long (including the handle). They're expensive and they're worth it. When you cut your cleaning time in half you'll appreciate how valuable they are.

Cleaning cloths. The best are pure cotton—white only. Used table napkins are perfect. You may be able to find them at a local linen service or hardware store. Don't substitute! Retire those old T-shirts, underwear, socks or hosiery, sheets, and most especially newspapers. Trying to use them to clean will make work and waste time. Keep a supply large enough that you will not run out once you've started to clean. When they are too worn for general use, use them on the oven or other heavy-duty jobs and discard them. Notice that we call them "cleaning cloths" so as not to suggest they're in tatters. We use retired cotton napkins that show some signs of wear, but they stop far short of being rags.

There are two other possible choices. The next best thing to cotton table napkins are 100 percent cotton, unfolded diapers. (If you have trouble finding them, they are still in the Sears mail order catalog.)

The third alternative is paper towels. It you're going to use them, don't pinch pennies. The best brand is Microwave Bounty paper towels.

Whatever your choice, we will refer to them as "cleaning cloths" from now on.

This is how to fold the cleaning cloths so they fit correctly in your carryall tray. It's simple but important, so please do it right.

① Fold in half ② Fold again ③ Fold top to bottom

Pump-spray furniture polish. We like Old English, and the pump-spray container carries well in the apron.

Furniture polishing cloth. You know, those yellow things you see in the stores—but get the untreated ones if you can. Use only for furniture polishing—not with blue juice or red juice.

Powdered cleanser. We use Comet. Use it to clean inside tubs, sinks, and toilets.

One-pint plastic container. (What's left over after you've eaten the expensive ice cream.) Use it in the bathroom to help rinse the hard-to-reach areas of the shower.

Whisk broom. Buy one with plastic bristles. Use it to clean the edges of carpets, especially on stairs, and for generalized brushing chores (e.g., between cushions on the couch).

50-foot extension cord on a cord caddy. Use a round cord because it resists knotting much more than a flat cord does. The cord caddy saves lots of

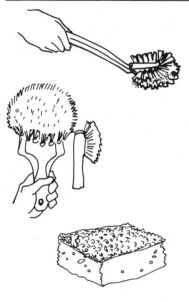

time by keeping the cord organized. One good knot can take as long to untangle as it takes to vacuum a whole room.

Toilet brush. We use brushes with stiff bristles to improve their scrubbing ability. Don't buy the brushes with bristles held in place by a twisted wire. They aren't worth the wire they're twisted in.

Tile brush. A large brush with stiff synthetic bristles. Used to scrub the tile and grout in the shower. Also used in the tub itself and in the bathroom sink.

White scrub pad/sponge ("white pad"). We use the one made by Scotch-Brite that has a white scrub pad on one side and a sponge on the other. Used when a cleaning cloth isn't strong enough.

Green scrub pad/sponge ("green pad"). Same as above except for the color. Use this pad *only* for cleaning the oven because it will scratch just about anything.

Mop. We use the sponge mop made by Continental Manufacturing Co. It is strong enough to really bear down without breaking. Also, the sponge is durable and replaceable. Keep it rinsed and clean between uses. It costs about $20 but is cheaper than the $5 grocery-store alternatives that will break whenever they are put to a real test.

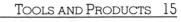

Floor cleaner/polisher. We use Mop & Glo. It works well to maintain certain floors while leaving a modest shine.

Ammonia. Use *clear* ammonia. Never "sudsy" or "detergent." Used to maintain floors not suited to cleaner/polisher (above).

Oven cleaner. Easy-Off is the simplest to use, and it works very well.

Rubber gloves. For cleaning the oven. The cheap ones rip immediately.

Vacuum cleaner—canister type. (The "Big Vac.") You don't have to go buy one if you don't have this type already. But next time you buy a vacuum, this is the one to get. It's easy to maneuver, it has a second motor in the beater head, and it quickly separates so the hose can be used for other tasks as the need arises.

Vacuum cleaner—portable. (The "Little Vac.") This second vacuum is necessary if you're going to work in a team because you will often need two vacuums going at the same time. This is especially true if you have hardwood floors anywhere in the house.

Miscellaneous. Pliers, a Phillips and a regular screwdriver, and a spare fanbelt for the Big Vac. Once you are on the job, you can't waste time looking for anything to solve little breakdowns.

A Final Word on Supplies

Since a few of these supplies may be hard to find, you can get information about any of them from us. (You can even ask us questions about any of the procedures of *Speed Cleaning*.) You won't have to wander around in the grocery store or hardware store trying to decide what product saves the most time; we know, so come to the source. At the present time we have ordering information about the following: work apron, red juice, blue juice, spray bottles, feather duster, mop, Old English furniture polish, toothbrush, razor-blade holder, scraper, cord caddy, and carryall tray. You can contact us at:

The Clean Team
2264 Market Street
San Francisco, CA 94114

KITCHEN MANUAL

Stock your carryall tray with the following items:

    1   powdered cleanser
    1   blue juice in a spray bottle
    1   red juice in a spray bottle
    1   white scrub pad/sponge combination ("white pad")
    1   green scrub pad/sponge combination ("green pad")
    1   feather duster
    1   oven cleaner
    1   pair of rubber gloves
    1   floor cleaner/polisher (or ammonia)
  10   cleaning cloths

Stock your Speed-Clean apron with:

    1   scraper
    1   toothbrush
    1   razor-blade holder with sharp blade
    2   plastic bags (as liners) with clips

Hand-carry the following:

> 1   sponge mop

The Kitchen Manual is designed to teach you how to clean any kitchen quickly, easily, and efficiently.

The Starting Point

Lean your mop just inside the door. Put your carryall tray on the countertop just to the right of the sink. The strategy for cleaning this room is to pick a starting point and proceed around the room clockwise, cleaning as you go—never backtracking, carrying all the tools and cleaners necessary in your apron.

This room is cleaned with lots of "pick up and replace" motions. For example, pick up your feather duster, use it, replace it; pick up the red juice, spray-and-wipe, replace it; pick up your toothbrush, etc. And when we say "spray-and-wipe" we mean that you'll be using a cleaning cloth and the red or blue juice. These motions will become smooth and effortless with practice. We've picked your starting place for you: where you put your tray.

We've drawn the floor plan for a sample kitchen and shown your trajectory through the room. "S" is where you start, and your path is

indicated with arrows. We have cleverly left a blank page so you can draw in your own kitchen floor plan after you've read this Kitchen Manual. It will help you visualize your proposed cleaning trip around your kitchen and especially help you to decide when to clean something in the middle of the room (like a work table, for example).

Getting Dressed

Tie your apron around your waist tightly. Check to be sure that the toothbrush and other tools are in their proper pockets. Hang the blue and red juice by their handles in your apron loops on the appropriate side. By "appropriate" we mean that if you put the blue juice on the left side, then *always* put it on the left side. This is so you can quickly reach for your red or blue juice without stopping to see which is which. It saves time. The tops of the spray bottles have an annoying tendency to come loose at the worst possible moments, spilling the contents everywhere. Avoid this potential catastrophe by automatically tightening the tops when you first pick them up. Stick your feather duster in your back pocket. Estimate the number of cleaning cloths you'll need and transfer them from the tray to your apron. At first, just guess by grabbing eight to ten cloths; as time goes on, you'll know how many you use. Finally check the illustration of you and your fully loaded apron. You're ready to move on.

Our Kitchen:

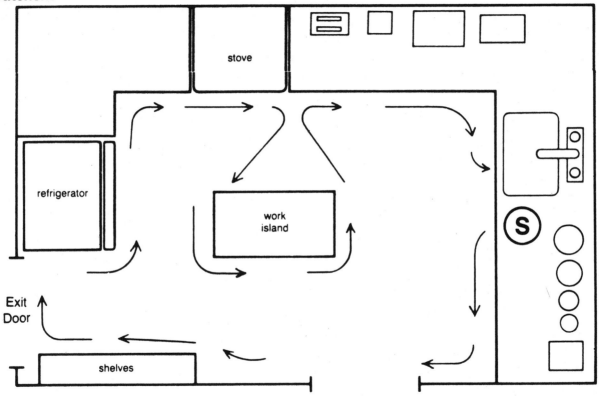

Draw your kitchen here:

Setting Up

Put any trash containers just outside the door or in the doorway, making sure they are out of the way (as much as possible) of the person who will be vacuuming. (Follow these directions even if you're working alone, since it is work you will do later and you want these items out of your way now.) Also, lay any throw rugs outside the door *flat* on the floor or carpet. That's *flat*: F-L-A-T. Flat. No corners tucked underneath. No rumpled mess. You're expecting the Vacuumer to do the rug, so you'd better not make him or her stop to flatten it if you want to avoid a brawl in the hallway. Similarly, the person collecting the trash is not going to take the time to rummage around the kitchen on your behalf. That's your job as the Kitchen Person. If you save someone else on the team a step you're saving yourself a step, and you're all going to the movies that much sooner. That's the idea.

Cupboards and Counters and Fingerprints

You are now going to start cleaning your way around our sample kitchen, *moving to the right, working from high to low* as you go. Above the counter are cupboards, and, since they are the highest, start with them. Usually all you have to clean are the fingerprints near the handles. Fingerprints need red juice, so grab your spray bottle from your apron loop and spray the prints lightly. Replace the spray bottle back on your apron loop as you wipe the area dry with your other hand.

You will generally be using two cloths. Carry the drier cloth over your shoulder so it's easy to reach. When that cloth gets too damp for streakless cleaning (chrome fixtures, glass, etc.) but still usable for general wiping, keep it in the apron pocket between uses, and sling a new dry cloth from your apron supply over your shoulder.

Cleaning fingerprints is a task where we are careful to apply Rule 4: "If it isn't dirty, don't clean it." If all you need to do is remove a fingerprint or two from an otherwise clean cabinet door, just spray the prints and wipe dry. Takes about 5 seconds. Don't haphazardly spray a large area of the cabinet door (which takes longer) and then have to wipe this larger area dry (which takes longer still). You've forgotten that all you wanted was that fingerprint and now you're cleaning the entire door. Stay focused on what you're doing, which is only the 5-second job of a quick spray-and-wipe of a fingerprint.

The places that often *don't* need cleaning are the vertical surfaces of the kitchen (the front of the cabinets, for example). The horizontal surfaces like the flat top of the counter will need cleaning every time. We have Newton to thank for this principle, plus his falling apple, gravity, and such. We are not proposing an excuse to be lazy or to skip things that need to be cleaned. Rather, the idea is to learn to be fast and efficient and aware of what you are doing. That includes *not* cleaning clean areas. After the fingerprints on the cabinet door, wipe the wall between the cabinets only if it has splatters. Otherwise it's not dirty, so don't clean it.

Spray and wipe the countertop area in front of you. (Pick up your carryall tray, spray and wipe the counter underneath it, and replace the tray.) Work from back to front, moving items to clean beneath and behind them. The "items" we're talking about are the sugar, flour, and tea canisters, the toaster, the food processor, and so forth. The spice rack may get moved to dust *behind* it, but that's all. Dealing with those individual containers is not light housecleaning, so just hit at the spice containers with your feather duster and save cleaning each spice bottle until some night you feel like doing it in front of the TV. Besides, the easiest way to clean a spice rack is to throw out all the old spices.

When moving items on the counter, pull them straight forward just far enough for you to wipe the counter behind them. Before you push these items back into place, now is the time to dust or wipe them. Dust them if that is all they need since that is the faster operation. Now push them back and continue on down to the drawers below.

Be sure to dust or wipe the tops of the drawer fronts as you come to them. Always check drawer handles and knobs for fingerprints (same rule as above, for cabinet doors).

The drawer knobs or the cabinet handles are often easier to clean by using your toothbrush in the tight areas rather than by trying to fit your cleaning cloth into a small or awkward place. The toothbrush is in your apron and is perfect for corners and other areas difficult to clean with a cloth alone. Use the toothbrush, your red juice, and then wipe dry. After you've cleaned them with the toothbrush, a quick wipe with a cloth will suffice for many future cleanings.

As you work your way around the kitchen, you will do a lot of spraying and wiping, spraying and wiping. Usually you can do this with the spray bottle in one hand and a cloth in the other.

When cloths get too wet or soiled, put them in the plastic-lined pocket. Or throw them to your tray if you're a good shot. But be careful: Cloths soaked with red juice may leave spots on the floor.

Get in the habit of always putting the spray bottles back in your apron loops, *not on the countertop*. We know it seems faster to leave them on the countertop, but it isn't. This may seem awkward at first, but do it—it's faster and it saves time.

Countertop Problems

So here you are, cleaning the counter with malice toward none and a song in your heart. Then you discover remnants of: (a) Saturday night's failed soufflé, (b) Sunday morning's blueberry pancake batter, and (c) other assorted stone artifacts that were once food. You are not amused. You took neither Chemistry nor Advanced Blasting Techniques in college. More to the point, you discover that when you spray and wipe these globs once, little or nothing happens. What to do?

First of all, when you come to a little nightmare on the countertop you have to resort to tools with greater firepower. Use your cleaning cloth most of the time since it normally will clean the countertop as it wipes up the red juice. When you encounter pockets of resistance like dried-on food, just move up to the tool of next magnitude—your white pad.

The white pad should be in your apron in a pocket lined with a plastic bag. When finished, always replace it in the same lined pocket. It doesn't matter that it gets dirty and begs to be rinsed, because you use it just to loosen dirt and not to remove it. Unless you just can't stand it anymore, don't rinse it until you get to the sink. Do try to get used to its being full of gunk.

Spray with red juice and agitate with the white pad until a mess of red juice and reconstituted five-day-old vegetable soup appears. This is the mess you need to learn to "see through" (Rule 5). To do this you need to be able to tell how the counter feels when you've cleaned through the goop to the surface without rinsing or wiping to take a look. If you have difficulty judging when you have scrubbed down to the actual bare surface (without wiping), try spraying a little red juice on a clean counter area next to the dirty area you are cleaning. By first rubbing your white pad on the clean area and then the dirty area you quickly learn to tell the difference by touch alone.

Another example of switching to a higher-horsepower tool is when you encounter food dried so hard that even a white pad takes forever to work. An example is drips of pancake batter that have dried to little bits of stone stuck to the counter. When you tried your white pad you found that you were rubbing one micron or so off the top of the dried pancake batter every swipe. You were using up MGT—Movie Going Time—again. When you first encounter the problem, better to put your cloth away, grab your scraper, and scrape the batter loose in a second or two. Replace the scraper and continue along your way. Be careful not to scratch the surface: Spray the surface first and keep the blade at a low angle. Remember, first use the cleaning cloth and increase the force or strength of the tool only as necessary (Rule 7).

Picture Glass, Window Glass, and Mirrors

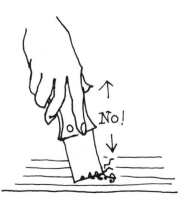

You need your blue juice and a dry cloth to clean these items, and since you are carrying them with you in your apron, there is no need to go back to the tray. To clean, spray lightly and evenly with blue juice and wipe with a dry cloth until the glass is dry. If you don't wipe it completely dry you will leave streaks—and if you don't use a very dry cloth, you are wasting time since it will take you longer to wipe the glass dry. When we say spray lightly, we mean it. Glass or a mirror cleaned with a quick light spray of blue juice gets just as clean as a mirror drenched in it. It just takes two or three times longer if you overspray! So don't. Replace the blue juice sprayer after each use—back where it was on your apron loop.

Cobwebs and Doors

As you continue around the kitchen moving to the right, working from high to low, look all the way to the ceiling each time you advance to check for cobwebs. Spiders like corners. When you see a cobweb, grab your feather duster from your back pocket, mow down the cobweb, replace the duster, and proceed. If you can't reach the cobweb, use the detached vacuum wand as an extension for the feather duster.

You're now going to pass a doorway in our sample kitchen. Another place to check for cobwebs as you pass by is the top of the door frame. Did you also check for fingerprints where people (especially very little people) seem to grab the door frame as they pass through? Good.

Open Shelves

Next are some shelves used to store cookbooks, pots and pans, and other kitchen stuff. Hit at the leading edges of these shelves with your feather duster only. (An alternative method is to thoroughly clean *one* shelf each time you clean the kitchen.) To clean a shelf, move all items to the right side and clean the vacant side, then move everything to the side you just cleaned and repeat. Finally, redistribute the items as they were. Or, if there are too many things on the shelf, move just enough items to the floor (or counter) so there is space to move the remaining items. When moving items to the floor (or counter) move them the least distance possible.

Refrigerator—Outside

Wipe the top first. Once you are cleaning this room on a regular basis you may be able to just feather-dust the top, which takes only a second or two. If the top of the refrigerator is used as a storage area, then just dust around all the items up there and treat it like the shelf we just described.

Clean the fingerprints from the outside of the fridge—and there are always some! Don't spray and wipe the entire refrigerator unless it needs it. Clean around the hinges, and the nameplate of the refrigerator—your toothbrush is the best tool. Open the refrigerator door to wipe and clean the rubber gasket. If it is dirty, make sure to use your toothbrush here also. Once you get many areas like this clean, you won't have to do them again for a long time: e.g., the refrigerator hinges, nameplate, rubber gasket, and cabinet and drawer handles.

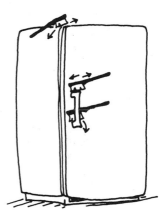

Wipe the refrigerator air vent (down near the floor) while the door is open—or if it is just dusty, use your feather duster. While the door is open, wipe fingerprints on top and on the side of the door near the handle. Also, clean off the line left by the gasket on the inside door lining. Check for easy or obvious little wipes that are needed on the visible areas of the interior shelves. Don't get carried away—it could take forever. (Instructions for a thorough cleaning of the inside of the refrigerator are in Chapter 8.)

The Stove Top

After you've cleaned the area above the stove—the hood usually needs to be sprayed and wiped—start at the back and work forward. Clean the vent filters by running them through the dishwasher occasionally. There are two main types of stove tops. Here is how to clean them.

Gas Ranges

These are easier to clean than electric ranges. Clean one side and then the other. First take the grills from the gas burners on the left side and set them on top of the burners on the right. Now spray and wipe the left side as necessary. You'll usually need your white pad here to get at the burned-on crud. If your pad won't work, use your scraper where possible, but the stove's curved edges often make this difficult.

If you are still unable to get the stove top clean, turn to your tray (next to the sink) and get your powdered cleanser. Use it *very lightly* in conjunction with your white pad. You will be using so little cleanser that you shouldn't even sprinkle it on the stove top. Instead, get a little of it from the top of the cleanser container with the wet edge of the white pad. If there is no cleanser on the top for you to use, then sprinkle a *small* amount on the stove top and dab with your white pad to pick up a little bit.

After you have cleaned the left side, replace the left burners and then move the burners on the right side to the *counter* immediately to the right of the stove. Now clean the right side the same way and replace the right burners.

Electric Ranges

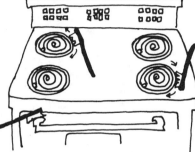

Usually there is a chrome or aluminum ring around the burners that needs attention. Normally you can clean around these rings (the edge of the ring where it meets the stove top) by spraying with red juice and using your toothbrush around each ring. Before you wipe, use your white pad to clean the metal itself. Now wipe dry with your cleaning cloth. As usual, work from back to front and from left to right.

If you can't get the stove top clean without moving the metal rings, then go ahead and lift up that particular ring (only that one) and spray and agitate with your white pad and wipe. If there is an accumulation under the burner that must be removed (*don't* if it's not much) then pull the burner up, remove the drip tray, and dump loose debris into your plastic-lined apron pocket. Use red juice and white pad to quickly clean, then wipe and replace. Don't try to make this drip tray look like new: If it's hopeless, it's smarter to throw it away and replace it once or twice or twelve times a year. If that drives you crazy, then use powdered cleanser to get them clean.

The Stove Front

Now that the top is clean, start down the front of the stove. The first little roadblock here is the row of burner control knobs. They can be cleaned by spraying with red juice and using your toothbrush on them and around their edges.

If you can't get this area clean without removing the controls, *first clean and wipe the knobs themselves while in place.* Then remove each one by pulling it straight out and setting it on the counter next to the stove *in the exact order* you took it off and in the same respective position it was in while on the stove. While the knobs are off, clean the area of the stove front you couldn't clean while the knobs were in place. Use red juice and white pad on this area and wipe it dry before replacing the knobs. This chore shouldn't have to be done often (unless the chef of the household is of the hysterical flinging school).

Open the oven door to get the oven side of the window. It can be cleaned with your razor blade. But be sure to spray the window first with red juice: It's easier to clean and it's also more difficult to scratch the glass when it's wet. This window should be cleaned inside and out even if you're not cleaning the inside of the oven. (Oven cleaning is the subject of Chapter 7.)

Wipe the rest of the front of the stove as necessary. Don't automatically clean the entire front of the stove. Remember that horizontal surfaces get dirty faster than vertical ones. Once again: If it isn't dirty, don't clean it.

The Middle of the Room

Now is the time we chose to turn around and do the work island in the middle of the sample kitchen. Not much to do here. Just spray and wipe the work space. The important thing is not to overlook it. Be sure to draw anything similar on your own floor plan (at the beginning of the Kitchen Manual) and show by arrows when you are going to clean it.

Toaster, Toaster Oven, Can Opener, and Microwave

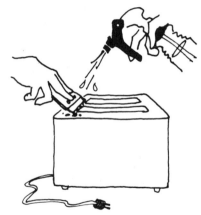

Return to the last bit of counter area to clean these items. You can make your 10-year-old toaster look like new by removing that burnt-on "brown" stuff with your razor *(gently)* and a white pad. Unplug the toaster and be brave. Wet the toaster liberally with red juice before you use the razor or you will scratch it. Just like the scraper, keep the razor at a low angle. Clean the rest of the toaster with red juice and your white pad, and use your toothbrush around the handles. Wipe the chrome dry and streakless (as you would glass). Clean the toaster oven similarly with red juice and use your toothbrush in those areas you are learning that your cloth won't reach. Also, use your razor blade on the (wet) inside glass of the toaster-oven door. Clean the can opener with red juice and use your toothbrush around the wheels as necessary. The microwave is easy. Spray and wipe inside and out.

A Little Reminder

Remember, don't "come back" to anything. Make sure everything has been attended to the first time around. If you have to go back to clean something you missed, you are doing something wrong, and you are wasting valuable time better spent elsewhere.

The Sink

You will finish the trip around the kitchen by ending up in front of the sink. If there are dishes in the sink, there shouldn't be. That is not *weekly* cleaning. It is *daily* cleaning. The dishes should be put in the dishwasher or otherwise dealt with before you do this weekly cleaning.

Clean above the rim of the sink with red juice (not cleanser) and a cloth—all except in the bowl of the sink itself. Every time you clean, use your toothbrush around the faucets and where the sink attaches to the counter. It makes a vast difference and it only takes a few seconds. Wipe clean and dry.

Now you need your powdered cleanser to clean the inside of the sink. (Use powdered cleanser *below the rim only,* or you'll spend too much time rinsing.) Conveniently enough, the cleanser is in your carryall tray right next to the sink on the counter—where you left it when you started your trip around the kitchen. Wet the inside of the sink. Sprinkle cleanser lightly on the bottom of the sink and then use your white pad to agitate the cleanser around the bottom and sides of the sink. Use your toothbrush to clean the little groove around the drain or garbage-disposal opening.

Rinse the sink thoroughly to remove the cleanser. Use your fingers to feel the sink bottom to be sure all the cleanser is removed. This is especially important since you may be using the sink as a bucket for some ammonia and water (see below) and some residual ammonia could react dangerously with the chlorine bleach in the cleanser. So rinse well.

Put the red and blue juice and the feather duster into your carryall. Take either ammonia or floor cleanser/polisher (see below) and put it in your apron pocket. See the carryall tray just outside the kitchen door (out of the path of the vaccuuming).

The Floor

First step is to vacuum the floor with the small vacuum and its large brush attachment. Vacuum into the room so the cord or exhaust is not dragging or blowing debris. Pick up large items that may clog the vacuum—like dog or cat food, dried lettuce leaves, carrot slices, nylon stockings, sleeping hamsters, etc. Pay particular attention to corners and to the grout on tile floors. Use a broom if no vacuum is available. (It can actually be faster.)

The next step depends on what type of floor you have. Use Method A (ammonia and water) if your floors are "no-wax" vinyl, hardwood floors coated with polyurethane, or tile floors (glazed, unglazed, or quarry). Use Method B (floor cleaner/polisher) if your floors are "wax" or "no-wax" vinyl or linoleum. (You may have noticed that "no-wax" vinyl floors made both lists. We use Method B because it protects the floor.) You choose which method is correct for your floor.

Method A. Ammonia and Water

Close the sink drain and run enough hot water into the sink to just cover the head of the sponge mop. Then add a small amount of ammonia (approximately 3 tablespoons). Rinse the mop in this solution and leave the mop almost dripping wet. Start in the corner farthest away from the exit door and clean a small area while distributing the water in the mop evenly over the area you're cleaning. When there isn't enough water left in the mop to continue cleaning, then go to the sink and repeat the process. As with all else, different degrees of cleaning are necessary. The dirtier area of the floor in front of the stove and refrigerator and sink requires harder scrubbing and *more frequent rinsing of the mop.* If the sink water becomes so dirty that you can't reasonably continue cleaning with it, just pull the plug (careful of the hot water), refill with water and ammonia, and continue cleaning. A small or standard kitchen that you are cleaning weekly should be able to be cleaned without having to empty and refill the sink. As you're mopping, use your scraper to loosen problem "globs" and your white pad to remove smears and heel marks.

If you pass the sink and have to come back to it before you finish the room, go ahead and walk over the area you just mopped. You'll take care of any footsteps as you leave the room for the last time.

Method B. Floor Cleaner/Polisher

Put the bottle of cleaner/polisher in your apron pocket. Rinse the mop with warm tap water, leaving it almost dripping wet. Go to the corner of the room farthest from the exit door. Apply a thin line of cleaner/polisher directly to the floor about 3 feet long. Apply from left to right, and don't apply closer than 2 feet to any wall or cabinet. Spread this line of cleaner/polisher as evenly as possible over an area of the floor approximately 4 feet by 4 feet, using enough pressure to clean as you go. Your purpose is to use your mop to pick up the dirt while leaving a little cleaner/polisher for a modest shine. If you loosen any debris that the mop doesn't pick up, be sure you pick it up yourself and put it in the plastic bag in the apron pocket. When using your scraper on blobs that the mop doesn't remove, loosen

them (once again at a low angle) and then either mop them up or pick them up and deposit them in your apron pocket. Repeat the process as often as necessary, and don't worry if you have to walk on the wet floor to return to the sink to rinse. We will remove any footprints when we leave the room the last time.

Finishing the Floor

The last time you are at the sink (after using either Method A or B), rinse your mop well and then remove as much water as you can. Lean it against the counter next to you (with the head in the air). Now rinse the sink out well and use a dry cleaning cloth to touch up the handles, the faucet itself, and any other splashes or drips outside of the sink. You needn't wipe the inside of the sink dry. Just leave it wet, rinsed, and clean.

Leave the kitchen, backing up as you go, mopping up any footprints you may have left. Put down one of your cloths to step onto when you leave the kitchen. Leave the mop in the kitchen doorway (upside down) near your carryall tray.

YOU'RE FINISHED!

If you're working alone, it's time to start the bathroom. If you're working in a team of two, report to your partner if he/she has finished the bathroom and begun dusting. If you have finished the kitchen first, then *you* start the dusting and give your partner a secondary assignment when your partner finishes the bathroom. (See Chapter 9, Team Cleaning.) If you're working in a team of three, go see the team leader.

Now go back to the page with our kitchen drawn in (p. 20). On the blank page, draw in your kitchen, including the sink, doors, shelves, stove, refrigerator, etc. Put an "S" to show where you will start by depositing your carryall tray. Put an "X" by the door where you will exit from, and an "R" where you'll put any throw rugs. Show your trajectory around the room with arrows. On pages 41 and 42 we have provided two summary pages; one stays in the book, the other can be torn out and taped up for you to refer to on your first adventure or two through the kitchen.

Kitchen Summary

(1) Lean mop just inside door. Put tray on counter-top just to right of sink. Hang red- and blue-juice bottles on apron loops. Put duster in back pocket and cleaning cloths in apron. Place trash cans and rugs outside. Spray-and-wipe around room to the right and top to bottom, starting above the tray. When too wet or dirty, place cloths in plastic apron pocket or throw them into tray.

(2) COUNTERTOP: Move items toward you just enough to wipe behind them. Dust or wipe and replace. Clean counter with red juice and cloth, white pad, or scraper.

( ) REFRIGERATOR (OUTSIDE): Use red juice. Open door and clean gasket and air vent.

( ) STOVE TOP: Do hood, then work from back to front, using red juice and cloth, white pad, scraper, or cleanser.

—Gas: Set left grills on right grills. Clean left side and replace left grills. Set right grills on counter. Clean right side and replace right grills.

—Electric: Try cleaning around burner ring in place with toothbrush. If that fails, remove the burner/ring assembly, clean, and replace. Dump debris into plastic apron pocket.

( ) STOVE FRONT: Try using toothbrush and red juice without removing knobs. If that fails, clean knobs in place, remove and wipe them, set them on counter, clean stove behind them, and then replace.

(6) SINK: Red-juice rim. Use toothbrush around base of faucet. Sprinkle cleanser into bowl only and use white pad. Rinse. Replace spray bottles and duster in tray. Set ammonia or Mop & Glo by sink and tray outside door.

(7) FLOOR: Vacuum with Little Vac. Choose cleaning method, depending on floor type:

—METHOD A: Fill sink with 4" hot water. Add 3T ammonia. With mop almost dripping, start in far corner. Rinse and rewet as needed. Use scraper on stubborn spots.

—METHOD B: Rinse mop with warm water. With mop almost dripping, start in far corner. Spread 3' line of Mop & Glo for each 10–15 sq. ft. Rinse, rewet, and repeat.

After both methods, rinse mop and lean it head-up against counter. Rinse sink and polish chrome. Mop up footsteps as you exit, stepping onto a cloth as you leave.

[NOTE.—Fill in Steps 3–5 depending on your own floor plan.]

Kitchen Summary

(1) Lean mop just inside door. Put tray on countertop just to right of sink. Hang red- and blue-juice bottles on apron loops. Put duster in back pocket and cleaning cloths in apron. Place trash cans and rugs outside. Spray-and-wipe around room to the right and top to bottom, starting above the tray. When too wet or dirty, place cloths in plastic apron pocket or throw them into tray.

(2) COUNTERTOP: Move items toward you just enough to wipe behind them. Dust or wipe and replace. Clean counter with red juice and cloth, white pad, or scraper.

( ) REFRIGERATOR (OUTSIDE): Use red juice. Open door and clean gasket and air vent.

( ) STOVE TOP: Do hood, then work from back to front, using red juice and cloth, white pad, scraper, or cleanser.

—Gas: Set left grills on right grills. Clean left side and replace left grills. Set right grills on counter. Clean right side and replace right grills.

—Electric: Try cleaning around burner ring in place with toothbrush. If that fails, remove the burner/ring assembly, clean, and replace. Dump debris into plastic apron pocket.

( ) STOVE FRONT: Try using toothbrush and red juice without removing knobs. If that fails, clean knobs in place, remove and wipe them, set them on counter, clean stove behind them, and then replace.

(6) SINK: Red-juice rim. Use toothbrush around base of faucet. Sprinkle cleanser into bowl only and use white pad. Rinse. Replace spray bottles and duster in tray. Set ammonia or Mop & Glo by sink and tray outside door.

(7) FLOOR: Vacuum with Little Vac. Choose cleaning method, depending on floor type:

—METHOD A: Fill sink with 4″ hot water. Add 3T ammonia. With mop almost dripping, start in far corner. Rinse and rewet as needed. Use scraper on stubborn spots.

—METHOD B: Rinse mop with warm water. With mop almost dripping, start in far corner. Spread 3′ line of Mop & Glo for each 10–15 sq. ft. Rinse, rewet, and repeat.

After both methods, rinse mop and lean it head-up against counter. Rinse sink and polish chrome. Mop up footsteps as you exit, stepping onto a cloth as you leave.

[NOTE.—Fill in Steps 3–5 depending on your own floor plan.]

BATHROOM MANUAL

Stock your carryall tray with the following items:

    1   powdered cleanser (with a plastic 1-pint container inverted over the top)
    1   white scrub pad/sponge combination (white pad)
    1   blue juice in a spray bottle
    1   red juice in a spray bottle
    1   toilet brush (in a plastic bag)
    1   tile brush
  10   cleaning cloths (folded)
    1   feather duster
    1   bleach in a spray bottle
    1   tile juice in a squirt bottle

Stock your Speed-Clean apron with:

    1   scraper
    1   toothbrush
    1   razor-blade holder with sharp blade
    2   plastic bags (as liners) with clips

Here is *your* bathroom. Looks a mess. Towels—some wet, some dry—in heaps everywhere. Mold growing in crevices. Toothpaste smeared on the mirror. Crud on the grout. Looks like a weekend job? The equivalent of three trips to the beach? Not at all! We'll have you out of here in just 15 minutes or less.

This room is typically used more often than any other in the house. It is also kept closed and damp. The dampness enables mold to flourish and traps and hardens dust onto surfaces.

The Starting Point

Walk into the bathroom. Do not be afraid. Face the tub. Put your tray down on the floor at the right end of the bathtub. The strategy for cleaning this room is to pick a starting point and proceed around the room clockwise, cleaning as you go—never backtracking, carrying all the tools and cleaners necessary with you in your apron. The bathroom is cleaned mostly with a spray-and-wipe, spray-and-wipe repetition. And when we say "spray-and-wipe," we mean that you'll be using a cleaning cloth and red or blue juice. We've picked your starting point for you: where you put the tray.

On page 46 we've drawn the plan for a sample bathroom and shown your trajectory through the room. "S" is where you start, with arrows indicating the proper path to take. We've left a blank page so you can draw in your own bathroom floor plan, but don't start drawing until after you've read this Bathroom Manual.

Getting Dressed

Tie your apron around your waist tightly. Check to be sure the toothbrush and other tools are in their proper pockets. Hang the blue and red juice by their handles in your apron loops on the appropriate side: If you put the blue juice on the left side, then always put it on the left side. This is so you can quickly reach for your red or blue juice without stopping to see which is which. It saves time. (Remember, the tops of the spray bottles have an annoying tendency to come loose at the worst possible moments, spilling the contents everywhere. Avoid this by automatically tightening the tops when you first pick them up.)

Don't put your feather duster in your back pocket or put cleaning cloths in your apron yet. In the bathroom, before you make your cleaning trip around the room (top to bottom, moving to the right), you are going to get three things out of the way: the tub/shower area, the sink (inside only), and the toilet (inside only).

Alert readers will notice that we're asking you to do a few chores before going around the room once, which seems to be a violation of Rule 1. It is. Without going into a lengthy explanation, we're asking you to work like this in the bathroom: (a) to avoid splashing previously cleaned areas, and (b) because you will be using brushes you normally don't carry with you. Don't think about it, just take our word for it.

"Our" bathroom:

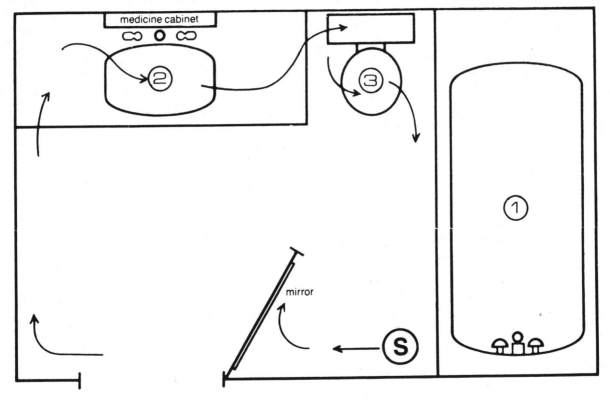

Draw in your bathroom here:

The Shower Walls

Step-by-step: how to move a rubber ducky

Before we deal with the shower area inside the tub, set any items that are around the edge of the tub out on the floor. Whenever you move anything like this, move it the shortest distance possible. For example, if there is a shampoo container or a rubber ducky, move it straight toward you and set it on the floor in front of the tub. There are two reasons for doing it this way: (a) It is faster. (b) When it comes time to replace the items, you automatically know where they were. Now that we've covered how to move a bottle of shampoo and a rubber ducky, let's move on.

First clean the shower walls around the tub—at least the areas that get wet when the shower is on. Use tile juice and the tile brush. (You have two brushes—one for the toilet and the other for the tub/shower and sink.) Although these are not in your apron, they are in your tray. And your tray (thanks to your observation of The Clean Team Rule 1) is right at your feet. The tile juice is in a plastic squeeze bottle that squirts instead of sprays. You don't want to inhale the fumes. The easiest way to apply the tile juice and clean the walls is to stand in the tub. Don't put tile juice on the areas that are already clean. (The higher part of the shower wall doesn't normally get wet during a shower and therefore doesn't need cleaning very often.)

Start by squirting some tile juice on the wall of the shower that is farthest from the faucet, and use your brush to evenly distribute it. Don't scrub. Continue around the shower, squirting the tile juice and spreading it around with the brush. Just distribute the juice with the brush until you've covered the area of the shower wall that needs cleaning. Tile juice works mainly by chemical action, so scrubbing is a waste of time at this point. It's got to sit there for a couple of minutes to loosen up the soap scum and hard water deposits. With the possible exception of the burned-on goop on the inside of an oven, there is nothing more resistant to cleaning than the hard water and soap scum deposits that you encounter in an ordinary shower . . . so let the tile juice work for you.

If there are shower doors, continue applying tile juice on the inside of the doors after you've finished coating the walls. Without getting out of the shower, replace the tile juice in your tray. Now start scrubbing the shower wall where you had first applied the tile juice. The brush works much better than your white pad because it digs into the grout between the tiles as well as the tiles themselves.

You'll be making a bubbly mess on the wall. Relax. It's just tile juice agitated by your scrubbing action, mixed with the soap and hard water deposits you are cleaning off. "See through" this mess (Rule 5) so you can tell when it's clean underneath and can quit cleaning one area and move on. You do this by learning to tell the difference between how your brush feels when it is cutting through the scum vs. when it is down to the clean bare surface. One way to learn this difference is to scrub a clean tile high on the wall and then scrub a dirty one. Notice the difference in friction between the two areas as you scrub. Or use your fingers on the clean vs. dirty areas to be able to feel the difference.

When you come to the soap dish, set the soap upside down (with the drier side down, so it won't slip away or leave a mess) in the nearest ledge corner of the tub. Clean the soap dish itself with your toothbrush: First scrape off the soap that has collected in the dish with the *handle* end of your toothbrush. Now brush out the remaining soap with the regular end of the toothbrush. Use red juice only if necessary. Final rinsing comes when you rinse the tub/shower area.

Shower Doors and Runners

After you have scrubbed the tile wall, continue on around and start the same action on the inside of the shower door. It's easier to "see through" the water and soap on the shower door to know when it is clean. If the brush isn't cleaning the doors well, increase the horsepower by switching to your white pad. (But only a white pad—never a green pad, which can scratch the glass.) If you have a shower curtain, skip ahead. (Don't try to clean it by hand: Throw it in the wash with a towel or throw it away.)

If the shower doors overlap, and you can't clean the area where they overlap by moving the doors, then spray some red juice on your white pad, wrap the pad around your scraper, and insert it in the small space in between the doors. Now move the scraper up and down to clean this area. Be careful as you work that the scraper doesn't get exposed because it could scratch the glass. Next, remove the scraper and substitute a rag for the white pad for a final wipe. The reason you use red juice here instead of tile juice is that it's a difficult area to rinse, and red juice doesn't require the rinsing that tile juice does.

If there is anything like paint or those 1960s daisy stickers on the shower door that can't be removed with the tile juice and white pad, use your razor blade. Be sure that the blade is sharp and use it properly (at a low angle) and you won't scratch the glass.

Time to step out of the tub. *Don't rinse yet.* If the bathroom is carpeted, put one of your cleaning cloths down before you get out so you can step out on it.

Next, take care of the shower door tracks (runners). Usually you can clean them with your toothbrush and red juice. If this doesn't work, use your scraper wrapped with a cloth. Move it back and forth inside the runner to clean it. Or fold your white pad in half and push it into the runner and move it back and forth. Again, *don't rinse yet.* There will probably be a lot of junk in the tracks and the temptation to rinse repeatedly will be strong. Cleaning the shower runners is one of those jobs that's a mess the first time, so don't expect it to be perfect yet. It becomes less of a chore each time you do it, eventually needing only a quick wipe.

The Tub

Next is the tub—leaving the shower runners, the shower doors, and the shower walls clean but covered with tile juice and whatever you have loosened up—all *unrinsed*. We haven't forgotten.

Get the powdered cleanser out of the tray and sprinkle it in the tub. Don't apply it anywhere but *in* the tub—not on the shower walls or faucets or shower head—just in the tub. Use the cleanser appropriately. If the tub isn't very dirty, don't use very much. While you are learning, resist your impulse to bombard the tub. Be conservative, since most powdered cleansers are abrasives and wear out porcelain. Also, it can take as much time to rinse it away as it does to scrub the whole tub. If you have a non-porcelain tub use a specialty product instead of powdered cleanser.

Use your tile brush to clean the tub, starting at the end away from the faucet and working your way toward it. Use the same "see through" method so you know when the porcelain under the foam and powder is clean. As necessary, use your toothbrush at the top of the tub where the tile starts. This is often Mold Heaven (or Hell). It comes off rather easily if you can get at it with your toothbrush. The problem arises when it is found growing in the tiny cracks in the grout and can't be removed with your toothbrush. Remove what you can. Later you can use bleach on the rest, but not until you are just about to leave the bathroom, since chlorine bleach is obnoxious and you don't want to breathe it if you can help it. Clean the shower head and faucets as you come to them, using your tile brush (and toothbrush) as necessary.

cleaning between tile & tub

Rinsing the Shower and Tub

Now everything inside the tub/shower area is a clean but foamy mess and you are ready to rinse. Put your *unrinsed* tile brush in the sink and leave it there while you rinse the tub/shower area.

Turn on the shower water to a comfortable temperature and pressure. Don't make it too hot or you'll fog up everything. If you are lucky enough to have a detachable shower head on a hose, rinsing is a pleasure. We happen to think that rinsing is a good enough reason to buy one . . . let alone being able to wash the dog with it. If you don't have one, aim the shower head back and forth to reach all the areas of the wall that have a coating of tile juice.

Completely rinse the walls before you rinse the tub. Rinse the shower walls from front (starting above the drain end) to back and from top to bottom. If there are areas that you can't reach with the shower spray, first try using your hand to deflect the shower spray to the area you need to rinse. If you still can't get it all rinsed, then use the plastic container that was over the top of the cleanser to catch water and throw it to those last nasty unrinsed spots.

After the walls are rinsed clean, rinse the tub—back to front toward the drain. *Use your fingers* to feel the bottom of the tub to know when all the cleanser is rinsed out. Don't depend on sight alone, as it is impossible to see a little leftover cleanser in a wet tub. The reverse, of course, is also true: If you leave a tiny bit of cleanser in the tub and wait for it to dry, it makes a dull film that you can see halfway down the block.

After you have rinsed the tub and there is no leftover cleanser or tile juice, turn off the water. Don't replace the items from around the tub yet, because if there's any mold left you will spray it with bleach in a few minutes.

The Sink—Inside

Reach into the sink where you had set your tile brush. Since it is still full of cleanser from the tub, use it as is to clean the sink. Be careful to keep the cleanser only *inside the bowl* of the sink, since it is difficult to rinse away. *Never* let powdered cleanser get onto an area that is hard to rinse . . . especially the top ledge of the sink around the faucets.

When the sink is clean, rinse out your tile brush in the sink and put it away in your tray. Rinse out the sink to finish that job. Don't dry and shine the chrome because you will do that in a few minutes. Grab the toilet brush and cleanser from your tray.

The Toilet—Inside

Sprinkle cleanser in and around the sides of the toilet bowl. Wet the toilet brush by dipping it in the toilet and sprinkle some cleanser on it. Start high in the bowl, on the inside upper rim. Move the brush in a circular motion and clean as deep into the bowl as you can. The water will quickly become cloudy, so be sure to start at the top and methodically work your way around and down the bowl. Don't forget under the rim! All kinds of gremlins live there.

As you washed the toilet bowl you were also washing and rinsing the toilet brush free of the cleanser you originally sprinkled on it. Shake excess water into the bowl and replace the brush in the plastic bag in your tray. Flush the toilet. That's out of the way!

Now it's time to clean around the room. Stick your feather duster in your back pocket. Estimate the number of cleaning cloths you'll need and transfer them from the tray to your apron. At first, try grabbing six to eight cloths. As time goes on, you'll know how many to use. You're ready to move on to the easy part.

Setting Up

Put any trash containers just outside the door (or in the doorway). Lay any throw rugs outside the door *flat* on the floor (or carpet). No corners tucked underneath. No rumpled mess. You're expecting the Vacuumer (who may very well be you) to do the rug later, so make it as easy as possible.

Mirrors

Start cleaning your way around the room moving to the right, working from high to low. Be sure to close the door as you go by. There is often a mirror on the inside of the door, and it needs to be cleaned. You need your blue juice and a dry cloth to do this, and since you are carrying these items with you in your apron, there is no need to go back to the tray.

Use your blue juice on the mirror behind the door, other mirrors, windows, and other glass items. To clean a mirror, spray it *lightly* and evenly with blue juice and wipe with a dry cloth until the glass is dry. Replace the blue juice sprayer after each use—back where it was in your apron loop.

You will generally be using two cloths. Carry the drier cloth over your shoulder so it's easy to reach. When that cloth gets too damp for streakless cleaning (mirrors, chrome fixtures, glass shelves, etc.) but is still usable for general wiping, keep it in the apron pocket between uses, and sling a new dry cloth from your apron supply over your shoulder. Throw your old cloth to the floor near your tray. If the bathroom is carpeted, put (or toss) the soiled cloths in your tray or you may ruin the carpet.

Fingerprints

The door also may have fingerprints on it that need a quick spray-and-wipe. Fingerprints need red juice, so get your juice, spray the prints, replace the bottle, and wipe the area dry.

Here's a task where we are careful to apply Rule 4: "If it isn't dirty, don't clean it." If all you need to do is remove a fingerprint or two from an otherwise clean door, just spray the prints and wipe dry. Takes about 2 seconds. Don't haphazardly spray a large area of the door (which takes longer) and then have to wipe this larger area dry (which takes longer still).

The places that often *don't* need cleaning are the vertical surfaces of the bathroom (the front of the toilet tank, for example). However, the horizontal surfaces (the flat top surface of the toilet tank, for example) will need cleaning every time.

Cobwebs

Train yourself to look all the way to the ceiling to check for cobwebs each time you advance. Spiders seem to especially like corners. When you see a cobweb, grab your feather duster from your back pocket, knock down the cobweb, replace the feather duster, and proceed. If you can't reach the cobweb, put the feather duster in a tube from the small vacuum.

Towels

Fold and rehang towels as you come to them. The towel racks themselves often need your attention—especially where the towel rack is attached to the wall. This is a place to use your toothbrush. A quick swipe with the toothbrush can clean such places much faster and better than your cleaning cloth alone.

Also clean the corners of the towel racks using your toothbrush and red juice and then wipe dry. After you've cleaned them with the toothbrush, a quick wipe with a cloth will suffice for many future cleanings.

The Medicine Cabinet

Wipe the very top with a damp cloth and then clean the mirror. If it has an outside shelf (usually with a supply of bathroom things on top of it—deodorant, toothpaste, perfume, etc.), move all the items to one side and spray and wipe the cleared area. Now pick up each item and wipe it clean as you move it to the other side. Then spray and wipe the second side and finally redistribute the items as they were. Don't open and clean the inside of the cabinet itself, as that's not part of weekly cleaning.

Below the mirror you'll probably find the toothbrush holder. Clean it with a quick spray-and-wipe. To clean the holes in the holder, put a corner of your cleaning cloth through each hole and pull up and down a couple of times.

The Sink—Outside Only

When you come to the sink use the red juice to clean around the faucets and the rest of the outside area of the sink—all but the inside of the sink itself (it's already clean, remember?). *Don't use powdered cleanser!!* Use the toothbrush around the base of the faucets each time. Use your white pad and red juice around the rest of the outside of the sink. Then rinse and wipe as usual. Use a dry cloth for a final wipe and shine of the chrome sink fixtures. Don't dry the whole sink . . . just the chrome.

Debris

Check below the sink and around the cabinet for fingerprints. Continue around the bath to the right, working from top to bottom. Pay particular attention to plants (dust them and then remember to put the feather duster back in your rear pocket), windowsills, pictures, moldings, etc. Don't miss the light fixture in the middle of the room. As you encounter loose trash,

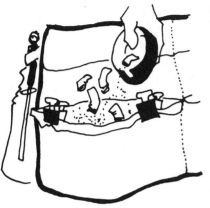

dump the debris into the plastic-lined pocket of your apron. (Don't walk to the trash can.)

Glass Trays

Another type of glass item you may encounter is a glass or mirrored tray filled with a collection of perfume or makeup items. Remove all the items from the tray, moving each item as short a distance as possible. Then spray and wipe the tray and replace each little bottle, wiping it as you move it back into place. Usually there's enough blue juice already in the cloth to do the job. If there is limited room to set things off the tray, you may be forced to put down the toilet lid to create a platform.

The Toilet—Outside

When you come to the toilet itself, start at the top of the tank and work down using red juice and a cloth. Once again, Clean Team Rule 4 applies: "If it isn't dirty, don't clean it." If the front of the toilet tank isn't dirty, don't take the time to "clean" phantom dirt. Don't forget to wipe the flushing handle as you go by.

When you get to the seat and lid, put them both in the "up" position and follow this sequence carefully. After you've done it a couple of times, you'll find that the explanation is much more complicated than the doing.

1. Spray the underside of the seat, and bring it down.
2. Spray the top of the seat. Don't wipe yet.
3. Spray the underside of the lid, and bring it down.
4. Spray the top of the lid. Also spray the hinges and the small flat area of porcelain on the far side of them.

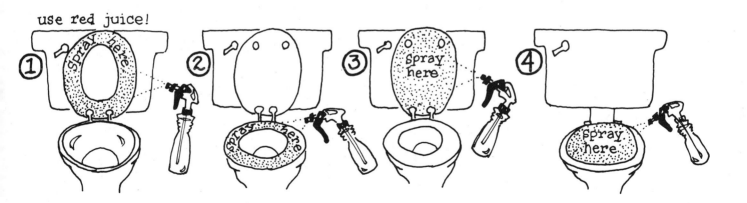

Hang your red juice on your apron loop and wipe in the reverse order that you sprayed. That means you start with the small porcelain area and hinges. Now start using your toothbrush where needed. The first target is around those hinges. Then wipe that area and the top of the lid dry. Raise the lid.

Use your toothbrush around the rubber bumpers and hinges (again). Wipe clean and dry. Don't worry about splatter on the clean porcelain yet. Wipe the top of the seat and raise it. Use the toothbrush again where needed and wipe dry. You're done with the lid and seat.

Now spray the top porcelain rim of the bowl. Tilt the seat and lid half forward with one hand and with the other retouch the hinge area of porcelain (catching those splatters). Push the lid and seat back fully upright and wipe the rim clean.

Clean all the way down the outside to the floor, using the toothbrush on areas such as where the toilet meets the floor and around those annoying little plastic caps. (The inside of the toilet is clean, so don't touch it at all.) If there is mold left at the base of the toilet after you've cleaned this area, leave it and spray it with bleach later.

The Floor Around the Toilet

Even though you haven't started to clean the floor yet, we prefer to be on our hands and knees, eyeball-to-eyeball with the toilet, only once. So clean the (uncarpeted) floor around the base of the toilet while you're there. Spray the floor around the entire base of the toilet with red juice and wipe it clean and dry. Remember that you are throwing the cloths into the far corner of the room (or into your tray) as they get too soiled or wet. Also remember not to throw soiled cloths on carpets—they might stain. If you have a carpeted bathroom, carry a whisk broom in your spare back pocket to brush the areas of carpet that the vacuum can't reach.

Shower Doors—Outside

Just before you finish your trip back to where you left your tray (on the floor at the right end of the tub), you will pass the shower doors. Clean the *outside* only with blue juice. Often all you need to clean are the fingerprints around the handle. You're just about done!

The Floor

You have been throwing the used cleaning cloths to the floor near your tray or in your tray if you're a good shot. Cloths that are too wet or dirty to be used to clean the floor should stay in your tray. Take several fairly clean and dry cloths to do the floor. Go to the far corner and (on your hands and knees) start spraying and wiping with red juice as you back out of the room. The proper technique is to spray an area lightly and evenly so that hairs and dust don't fly around. Then wipe up with your loosely folded cloths in a deliberate, methodical side-to-side movement (sort of a flattened "S" pattern). As you pick up hair and debris, carefully fold the cloth to trap the hairs you've collected so far and continue. When one cloth is too dirty or full, use another cloth. You don't have to dry the floor, but wipe it and turn your cloths often to avoid making streaks.

Bleach

As you're cleaning the floor on your way to the door, decide if you need to spray bleach on any mold in the tub/shower area. If so, get your bleach and a rag out when you reach the tub and your tray.

Bleach destroys just about everything, so treat it like strontium 90. Hold a cloth under the spray nozzle to catch any drips. Set the spray adjustment of your bottle to "stream" instead of "spray" so you minimize the amount of bleach in the air that you might inhale. Apply it as a liquid dribble directly on moldy areas. Wipe off any bleach that gets on the chrome fixtures immediately. Bleach dripping off chrome turns the tub's porcelain black. The discoloring isn't permanent, but it can be awfully discouraging. When through, drape the same cloth over the spray nozzle to catch any drips as you take your tray through the house. One drip on a carpet will make a little white spot that lasts forever! Keep the top of the bleach spray bottle covered with a cloth at all times except when you're using it. Also aim the nozzle toward the center of the tray. Changes in room temperature can make bleach ooze out. So can pressure from other objects in your tray. The first time you dribble bleach on your carpet you'll realize we were not being too fussy, but it will be too late.

Escape

Replace the covered bleach bottle in your tray and set the tray outside the bathroom. Now is the time to replace all the items that were around the edge of the tub: the soap back into the tray, the shampoo and the rubber ducky back to their spots. Now continue cleaning the floor as you back out . . . spraying and wiping until you have worked your way out of the bathroom.

The last few touches. Spread one dirty cloth on the floor and place the other dirty cloths in the center. Tie opposite corners of the bottom cloth together. This is called a "rag-a-muffin." Don't move the trash or the carpet that you previously set outside. They will be taken care of after the carpet is vacuumed and it's time to empty the trash.

YOU'RE FINISHED!

Spare Bathrooms

If there is a second bathroom that is used daily, go clean it now in exactly the same way. If there is a spare bathroom not often used, clean it according to the "If-It-Isn't-Dirty-Don't-Clean-It" rule and use only as much energy as needed: Don't automatically clean the mirrors if they're not dirty. Don't spray the door for fingerprints if none exist. Dust items that you might normally wipe. If the tub/shower hasn't been used, just wipe it quickly with a damp cloth, or spray and wipe with blue juice to remove dust. If you do this it will be just as clean as the one that is used more often, but it will only take you a couple of minutes.

Different Bathroom Floor Plans

If there is a shower stall only and no tub, then treat the shower stall as you would the tub. In other words, set your tray by the right side of the shower when you first enter the bathroom.

If there is a tub separate from a shower stall, start by setting your tray down as we just taught you. Then clean the tub, the shower stall, the sink (inside), and the toilet (inside). Finally, clean around the room as previously discussed.

Floor Plan and Summary

Now it's time to go back to the blank space left for your floor plan. Draw in your own bathroom and show your starting spot and the direction you'll clean in as we did in the sample.

On the next two pages you will find identical summary pages of the Bathroom Manual. Cut out one of them to tape up in the bathroom. It will help you your first few times cleaning.

Bathroom Summary

(1) Put carryall tray on floor at right end of tub. Hang red- and blue-juice bottles on apron loops. Put duster in back pocket and cleaning cloths in apron. Place trash cans and rugs outside. Spray-and-wipe around room to the right and top to bottom. Throw cloths in tray when too wet or dirty.

(2) SHOWER: Blue-juice outside of shower doors. Remove items in shower and put on floor. Grab tile brush and tile juice and step into tub. (Make sure it's dry and keep your tennies on.) Start at end away from faucet and squirt tile juice on shower walls, nozzle, and doors—one section at a time. Spread with brush, then squirt next section. Don't scrub yet. Replace tile juice in tray. Scrub walls and doors with tile brush in same order. Use white pad or razor blade, if needed. Leave tile brush in tub and step out. *Don't rinse yet.* Use red juice, cloth, white pad, and/or scraper on shower door tracks. Don't rinse!

(3) TUB: Sprinkle cleanser in tub and use tile brush, starting at end away from faucet. Clean faucet as you reach it. Put unrinsed tile brush in sink.

(4) RINSING: Rinse shower walls, starting near drain. Rinse tub, starting at end away from drain. Don't wipe yet.

(5) SINK (INSIDE): Use tile brush as is on sink bowl. Rinse out brush in sink and put in tray. Rinse sink. Polish chrome in sink and then in shower.

(6) TOILET (INSIDE): Sprinkle cleanser inside bowl. Wet toilet brush, sprinkle cleanser on it, and clean in a circular direction (high to low). Shake excess water from brush and replace. Flush.

( ) SINK (OUTSIDE): Red-juice faucets and sink except for bowl, using white pad and toothbrush. Wipe with cloth, but don't polish chrome yet.

( ) TOILET (OUTSIDE): Red-juice tank. Raise lid and seat. Spray underside of seat and lower it. Spray top of seat and underneath lid. Lower lid and spray top of it. Wipe in reverse order. Spray and wipe floor around base of toilet.

(9) FLOOR: Starting at far corner, use red juice and two cloths on floor: one to push debris forward, and the other to wipe clean. Spray bleach on mold in tub/shower/toilet areas, and replace shower items as you pass by. Make a "rag-a-muffin."

[NOTE.—Fill in Steps 7 & 8 depending on your own floor plan.]

Bathroom Summary

(1) Put carryall tray on floor at right end of tub. Hang red- and blue-juice bottles on apron loops. Put duster in back pocket and cleaning cloths in apron. Place trash cans and rugs outside. Spray-and-wipe around room to the right and top to bottom. Throw cloths in tray when too wet or dirty.

(2) SHOWER: Blue-juice outside of shower doors. Remove items in shower and put on floor. Grab tile brush and tile juice and step into tub. (Make sure it's dry and keep your tennies on.) Start at end away from faucet and squirt tile juice on shower walls, nozzle, and doors—one section at a time. Spread with brush, then squirt next section. Don't scrub yet. Replace tile juice in tray. Scrub walls and doors with tile brush in same order. Use white pad or razor blade, if needed. Leave tile brush in tub and step out. *Don't rinse yet.* Use red juice, cloth, white pad, and/or scraper on shower door tracks. Don't rinse!

(3) TUB: Sprinkle cleanser in tub and use tile brush, starting at end away from faucet. Clean faucet as you reach it. Put unrinsed tile brush in sink.

(4) RINSING: Rinse shower walls, starting near drain. Rinse tub, starting at end away from drain. Don't wipe yet.

(5) SINK (INSIDE): Use tile brush as is on sink bowl. Rinse out brush in sink and put in tray. Rinse sink. Polish chrome in sink and then in shower.

(6) TOILET (INSIDE): Sprinkle cleanser inside bowl. Wet toilet brush, sprinkle cleanser on it, and clean in a circular direction (high to low). Shake excess water from brush and replace. Flush.

( ) SINK (OUTSIDE): Red-juice faucets and sink except for bowl, using white pad and toothbrush. Wipe with cloth, but don't polish chrome yet.

( ) TOILET (OUTSIDE): Red-juice tank. Raise lid and seat. Spray underside of seat and lower it. Spray top of seat and underneath lid. Lower lid and spray top of it. Wipe in reverse order. Spray and wipe floor around base of toilet.

(9) FLOOR: Starting at far corner, use red juice and two cloths on floor: one to push debris forward, and the other to wipe clean. Spray bleach on mold in tub/shower/toilet areas, and replace shower items as you pass by. Make a "rag-a-muffin."

[NOTE.—Fill in Steps 7 & 8 depending on your own floor plan.]

DUSTER MANUAL

Stock your carryall tray with the following items:

  1   blue juice in a spray bottle
  1   red juice in a spray bottle
  1   whisk broom
10   cleaning cloths
vacuum attachments
  1   feather duster
  1   extension cord (on a cord caddy)
  1   furniture polish and cloth
  1   emergency kit:
      2 screwdrivers (Phillips and regular)
      1 pliers
      1 spare vacuum belt

Stock your Speed-Clean apron with:

  1   scraper
  1   toothbrush
  1   razor-blade holder (with a sharp blade)
  1   plastic bag (as a liner, with clips)

Definition

The Duster's job is to start cleaning the house except for the kitchen and bathroom. This work is drier than the work in the kitchen and bathroom: less spraying and wiping. There are several rooms involved, but they go faster, and there are no floors to wash—except wiping up an occasional drip of something. If you're going to work in a team, the Duster is also the team leader. But we'll get to that in Chapter 9.

Strategy

The strategy here is similar to the one for the kitchen and bathroom: Start in one place and then work your way through the rooms without back-tracking, using The Clean Team Rules.

As before, work from high to low. For the Duster, this instruction takes on additional importance: Dust follows a relentless gravitational path downward, diverted only temporarily by air currents. Unless you have a healthy respect for this physical reality you will find yourself redoing your work constantly. You will have an understandable human impulse first to dust what's right in front of you or what's interesting or what's easy to reach. Instead, train yourself to look *upward* toward molding, tops of picture frames, and light fixtures first, always checking for cobwebs.

Finish each area as you pass by. Do all the dusting, polishing, wiping, brushing, wet-cleaning, and tidying you need to do in an area as you pass through it. Change tools and cleaning supplies as needed: If you are dusting happily along with your feather duster and happen upon raspberry jam smeared on the top of the TV set, *quick!* Pop the feather duster into your back pocket with one hand as you reach for the red juice with the other. Spray with one hand as the other reaches for the cleaning cloth. Wipe with one hand as the other replaces the spray bottle on the apron loop. Then stow the cloth back in your apron as the other hand reaches for the feather duster and you are on your way again. A true blitz—a sign that you are mastering what you are doing. For pity's and time's sake, don't go around the room once to dust, then to polish, then to tidy things, etc.

Whether or not you are working with others, part of your strategy is to reduce the work load of the Vacuumer. (The Vacuumer will normally be someone else if you are working with another person.) Throughout the Duster Manual, we'll suggest ways you can shorten vacuuming time by doing what would have been some of the Vacuumer's work as you dust your way through the house.

Pay attention. Be alert to smarter ways of doing what you're doing. When you shave off a minute or two each time you clean—not by rushing, but by smarter cleaning—that's what it's all about.

Our floor plan:

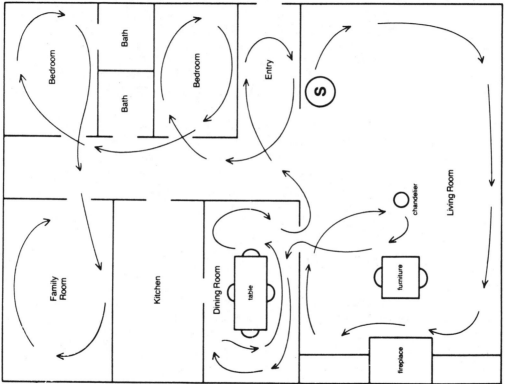

Draw in your floor plan here:

The Floor Plan

Since your home or apartment is unique, and since there are so many possible floor plans, we are going to discuss a typical one. Then after you've read this manual, you'll draw a floor plan of your own home and (using ours as a guide) chart your way through your home. So, before you even pick up your feather duster, you'll know where you're going to start, where you're going next, and where you'll finish.

First, though, we'll work our way through the rooms a Duster is likely to encounter—in this case, in our sample home. As we go, we'll explain cleaning methods and techniques to be used in each room and on the furniture, fixtures, and other items. Since there are so many possible arrangements, we do not suppose we're covering them all. We believe, however, that by learning our techniques for these typical rooms you'll know how to approach items not specifically mentioned here or items arranged in a different order in your home. We know this because it is much more important that you follow the *rules of cleaning* we're teaching rather than learn "hints" about specific items. You use the same technique on a $5,000 Baccarat crystal centerpiece as on a 50¢ garage-sale vase. You may breathe a little differently, but you clean them the same way.

Our sample living room, dining room, entryway, and hall have rugs on a hardwood floor. The bedrooms and master bath have wall-to-wall carpeting.

Getting Dressed

Put your apron on and load it from your tray, putting red juice on one side and blue juice on the other. Put the furniture polish and its dedicated cloth in your apron. Put your feather duster in a back pocket handle first, of course! The whisk broom goes in the other back pocket. Take six to eight cleaning cloths and put them in the apron also. (Next time you clean, you'll know better how many cloths to grab.)

Managing Cleaning Cloths

As you start to spray and wipe your way around the room, carry the drier cleaning cloth over your shoulder so it's easy to reach. When that cloth gets too damp for streakless cleaning (mirrors, picture glass, etc.) but is still usable for wiping, rotate it to the apron pocket and sling a new dry cloth from your apron over your shoulder. Use the damp cloth for wetter cleaning jobs like fingerprints, spots on the floor, and windowsills, for example. When that cloth in turn gets too damp or dirty and is no longer usable even for wiping, store it in the bottom of your lower right apron pocket.

Managing the Feather Duster

Approach most situations with your feather duster in one hand and the other hand free. Shift quickly to heavier-duty cleaning options as the situation demands, and gradually you'll notice you're beginning to do so smoothly and to anticipate your next move.

DEAD STOP!

If you use proper technique with the feather duster, you will move most dust quickly from wherever it was to the floor, where it will be vacuumed away. (High to low—Rule 3.) Poor technique will throw a lot of dust into the air and contribute to the poor reputation already suffered by feather dusters.

Most dusting motions are fast, steady motions over the surface being dusted—a picture frame, for example. At the end of the dusting motion (i.e., at the end of the picture frame), bring the duster to a dead stop. *Don't let the feathers flip into the air at the end of a stroke, thereby throwing all the dust into the air, where it will stay until you've finished cleaning and then settle back on all the furniture you've just finished cleaning.*

By coming to a dead stop at the end of each stroke, you will give the dust a chance to cling to the feathers. To remove the accumulated dust from the feathers, regularly hit the feather duster smartly across your ankle. The object is to get the dust to settle on the floor where it will await vacuuming.

The Starting Point

Set your tray on the floor at the starting point (point "S") on the floor plan (p. 74). You're going to start by cleaning the living room.

The Living Room

Cobwebs

Rule 3 says to work from top to bottom, so the first thing to do is to look up and check for cobwebs. Use your feather duster to remove them. If they're out of reach, stick your feather duster in the end of one or two lengths of vacuum wand. Then do a quick tour of the whole room, as it's too time-consuming to put down and pick up this makeshift apparatus more than once. Kill all spiders. Or catch them and let them loose outside if you're a pacifist or if they beg for mercy.

Fingerprints

Dust door panels or trim with the feather duster. Clean fingerprints around the doorknob with red juice (spray and wipe). Then, with red juice and cloth still in hand, clean the light switch next to the door. Move to the right along the wall, dusting everything from cobwebs on the ceiling to dust on the baseboards with long "wiping" motions of the feather duster.

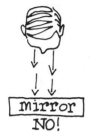

mirror
NO!

mirror
YES!

Remember to stop dead at the end of each swipe. Shift to wet cleaning (red juice, blue juice, or polish) only if you need to—as Rule 7 says.

Mirrors and Pictures

Picture glass only needs wet cleaning a few times a year. To test for cleanliness, run your *clean* and *dry* fingers lightly over the glass. Any graininess or stickiness means clean it. If it needs it, wet-clean by spraying blue juice lightly and evenly and then wiping dry. Wipe it *dry*, not just until it looks dry. The difference equals a streak: Glass begins to *look* clean as you're wiping it even though it's still slightly wet with blue juice. Wipe until it's completely dry. Trust us.

Wipe in broad movements, taking care to wipe the corners well. Don't wipe in small circles or random excursions. Also, stabilize the frame with one hand—*firmly*, don't be halfhearted—while you wipe with the other. If you don't stabilize it, it may fall or leave scratches on the wall from the frame moving as you clean.

The woods are full of people who can do a slow and mediocre job of cleaning glass. Our goals are higher, and one of the things that makes the greatest difference is checking your work. If you look head-on into the glass you will see a reflection of your own sweet face but you may miss 80 percent of the dirt on the surface. Check it from as narrow an angle as you can.

Once you have cleaned a picture frame or mirror, it probably won't need a thorough wet-cleaning again for weeks or even months. Dust it every week or so on the top of the frame and occasionally even the glass itself.

Wall Marks

As you dust, check the walls for marks and fingerprints. Use red juice on wall marks of all kinds. Before you move to the next section of the wall, look all the way to the floor (especially when there is a wood or tile floor) to check for little dried-up spills that should be wiped away.

End Table—Surface

Clean *above* the end table first. With wiping motions of the feather duster, dust the lamp shade, bulb, lamp, and then the objects on the table. The surface of an end table is rarely touched, so there is no need to use furniture polish every week. Just use your furniture-polish cloth without extra polish. By "polish" we mean either wax or oil—an important distinction to make, it turns out, as the two do not get along well on the surface of furniture. If you've been using an oil polish ("lemon oil," "red oil," etc.) continue using it. Otherwise use the Old English from your apron pocket—a type of liquid wax.

End Table—Objects

When cleaning an object-laden table just work from top to bottom again. Use your feather duster first (on lamps and objects on the table), then a damp cloth (on objects that need more cleaning), and then the polishing cloth (on the table itself).

Use caution. Cleaning and moving small items on shelves and tables is the scene of most accidents for dusters. A few guidelines will avoid most

accidents: Most important, pay attention to what's in front of you. Use both hands to move anything top-heavy or irreplaceable, or anything composed of more than one piece (e.g., a hurricane-lamp base with a glass lantern on top). It's almost never wise to move something on a pedestal by pushing the pedestal. Steady the top piece with one hand and grab the pedestal with the other. You usually get to make only one mistake with such things. And keep a wary eye out for heavy objects: *Do not*, oh *do not*, slide them across the surface of furniture. Scratches will follow in their path without fail or mercy.

Dust Rings

Our end table is on a wood floor, so use your feather duster to wipe the floor around the legs and underneath it to save time for the Vacuumer. By dusting these areas where the vacuum would leave rings or where the vacuum can't reach, you are speeding up that job, since the Vacuumer won't have to stop to do it.

Couch

Fabrics vary greatly in characteristics that affect cleaning strategy. If you're lucky, your furniture will need only a quick swipe with the whisk broom. At the other extreme are fabrics that hair will cling to until you pluck if off like a surgeon. In the middle are a great number of fabrics that can cooperate reasonably and respond to your whisk broom. Every so often even the most agreeable of fabrics could use a good vacuuming, however, to remove accumulated dust. The frequency of vacuuming varies depending on how dusty your environment is and how sloppy you are. If you like to eat crackers while sitting on your couch or if the cat sleeps there, you will overwhelm the capacities of the whisk broom and will have to call in the vacuum regularly. But not now. *First finish* dusting and polishing.

Back to our sample couch, however, which has pet hair and cookie crumbs on it. Clean from the top down, using your whisk broom. You will be tempted to start with the cushions, as they are easiest to deal with. Resist. First, starting with the left side of the couch, whisk the crumbs and hair from the top, back, and sides. (Careful not to make work for yourself by whisking debris onto the clean end table.) Whisk down and toward the cushion.

Should you clean under the cushions? Ah, the eternal question asked by reluctant dusters! The answer lies under those very cushions. Lift up a cushion or two and peek. You will know instantly. If it needs a thorough cleaning underneath, set the left cushion on the one next to it to get it out of the way while you whisk out that area. Then move to the next section and (starting once again at the top of the couch) repeat the process. If the area under the cushions only needs a touch-up, just tilt the cushion up for a quick swipe with the whisk broom. Leave the tops of the cushion for the Vacuumer, who can do them much faster.

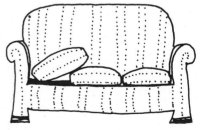

To signal the Vacuumer that the cushion tops *only* are to be vacuumed, leave a cushion overlapping the next one. The large vacuum has a beater

brush that is safe for most fabrics. You simply lift the beater brush up to the couch cushions and vacuum away. No further vacuuming is necessary as long as you have removed the hair and crumbs from the rest of the couch. Keep in mind that you want to do everything possible to make vacuuming easier. These steps greatly reduce vacuuming time.

Be careful. Vacuuming fabric with the beater brush can catch certain loose fabrics, could catch tassels or strings, could damage certain delicate fabrics, or may speed wear of your couch. If you prefer to avoid any risk, use the small vacuum.

If the amount of pet hair on the couch demands that the *entire* couch be vacuumed, then don't whisk it at all. It can be vacuumed with the small vacuum after the dusting. The signal to remind yourself or a partner to vacuum the *entire* couch is to stand one cushion straight up.

To signal the Vacuumer to clean *under* the couch, move one corner of the couch forward. If the couch is the sort that sits flush to the floor, it doesn't need to be moved often, since it's almost impossible for dirt to get under it.

Plants

Continuing top to bottom and left to right, you come to a large potted plant in the corner. Dust the plant with the feather duster top to bottom. On broad-leaf plants, support a leaf with one open hand while you dust with the other so the stem doesn't snap. Pick up the dead leaves, which often clog the vacuum, and put them in the apron trash pocket. Our sample plant is close to the wall and too heavy to move easily, so, with the polish rag, dust the hardwood floor around and behind it where the vacuum can't reach—once again, saving the Vacuumer time.

Drapes and Window Frames

Next is a wall with windows. With your feather duster, dust the top of the drapes and curtain rods for cobwebs. Working from top to bottom, dust all the window frames. Don't use a feather duster on wet windows unless you want to ruin your day. (A wet feather duster is pitiful.) Often in the winter you'll have to wipe with a cloth because the frames are wet. Then dust the windowsill.

Leather Chair

Particles of dust, sand, and grit work their way into leather and wreak havoc with the finish. The whisk broom is excellent for dusting leather furniture, especially if the upholstery is tufted and has buttons or piping. And use your toothbrush if the cracks and crevices are dirty: Keep both in hand, because with the whisk broom you can brush away particles the toothbrush dredges up. (Brush/swipe, brush/swipe, brush/swipe. . . .)

Bookshelves

Next is the fireplace wall with bookshelves on each side. Dust the tops of the books if there is enough space, and dust the exposed edges of the shelves with long wiping motions of the feather duster. Remember to shake the dust out of the feather duster at regular intervals near floor level by whacking it across your ankle.

Dust very ornate objects (e.g., candlesticks) with small squiggly motions of the feather duster so the feathers get into all the little places.

Do not dust the hearth because you will get soot on your feather duster and ruin it. Leave it for the small vacuum. If the room had wall-to-wall carpeting, you would wipe the hearth with a cloth so the Vacuumer wouldn't have to bring in the small vacuum just for the hearth. (See Chapter 6, Vacuuming.)

squiggle squiggle squiggle squiggle

Middle of the Room

You now come to the entrance to the dining room. Before leaving the living room, dust the molding on the small section of wall between the door to the entry hall and the door to the dining room. Move to the center of the room and dust the chandelier with the feather duster (squiggly motions).

Polishing the Table

On the carpet in front of the fireplace is a card table with four chairs that have been well used. Moving around the table, first pull each of the chairs away from the table and dust each one in turn. Do this with your polishing cloth in one hand and a feather duster in the other. Use the polishing cloth on the tops and arms of the chairs and the feather duster on the frame and slats. Leave the chairs away from the table to make it easier for the Vacuumer to maneuver.

To polish a small tabletop, spray on polish in a thin and even coat. Begin to wipe immediately, because polish left in place even for a minute or so begins to eat into the finish. (If that starts to happen, spray on more and wipe like mad.) *Wipe in the direction of the wood grain*. This is more shrewd than superstitious: Streaks left by imperfect polishing will be camouflaged by blending in with the wood grain if you rub in that direction. Wipe with your polishing cloth folded into an area as large as your hand—not mushed into a ball—so you make maximum use of each swipe. *(Saves time.)* As you rub, the polish will spread out evenly and begin to dry. When it is almost finished drying, flip the cloth onto its back—which should be kept *dry*—and buff the finish to a shine. Make big sweeping movements to save time. When the table exceeds your arm length, spray half at a time. (The table, that is, not your arm.) Don't press down hard as you buff: It's harder work and you can scratch the surface even with polish. Finally, check for streaks and missed spots, and deal with them with the driest part of the cloth.

Dining Room

Enter the dining room from the living room and begin dusting above the doorway, working from top to bottom as always. In the first corner is a plant: Use your feather duster as you did earlier.

Mirror-top Buffet

Across the back wall is a mirror-top buffet with liquor bottles on top.

Move the bottles to the right side and spray and wipe the vacated area. Use a blue-juice-sprayed cloth to clean the bottles as you replace them. If you encounter cigarette butts or other debris, remember to deposit same in your apron trash pocket. *Do not* walk around looking for a trash can! Clean the other side of the mirror-top and continue. Our buffet sits on the hardwood floor on short legs. The vacuum can get underneath, but use the feather duster around the legs to prevent dust rings.

Dining-room Table

Polish the dining-room table each time unless it hasn't been used at all. It saves the most time to polish half of the table, dust the chairs closest to you, polish the other half of the table, and then finish the chairs. The point is to minimize retracing your steps. A good brushing is all most chair seats need. Don't forget to dust the chair rungs or the legs themselves if they curve outward near the tip. While you're down there, check to see if either the pedestal or crossbeams of the table need dusting too.

The Hallway

Go into the entry hall and dust in the same way, beginning above the door and working from top to bottom around the entry. The table is unused and requires only the feather duster for the objects and the polishing cloth for the table. Use the feather duster around the legs of the table again.

Enter the hall and continue in the same top-to-bottom manner but alternately dust and wipe sections of *both walls* as you move down the hall. Don't do one side and then the other; you waste time retracing your route.

The Bedrooms

Enter the first bedroom off the hall. Begin in the same manner, above the door, moving to the right. Pull the foot of the bed away from the wall to indicate if the Vacuumer should clean under it this time. As the Duster, you are in charge of knowing which chores are to be rotated—and which rotation is to be done this time. An example is vacuuming under the bed, which may not need to be done every week but can't be ignored forever either. The same applies to heavy furniture (like the couch), and some high molding and other difficult areas to vacuum.

Desk

The desk in our sample room is so close to the corner that the head of the vacuum won't fit, so use the whisk broom to dust and fluff that section of carpet next to the desk. (Remember, this is wall-to-wall carpet.) This will keep the carpet pile from looking dusty. You can vacuum this spot every few months when you move the desk to vacuum behind it. Also, set any trash cans as close to the doorway as you can without interrupting your trip around the room.

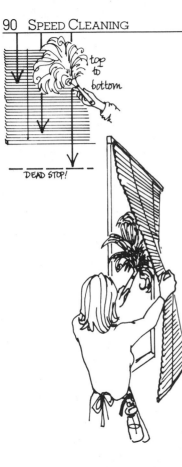

Telephone

Only rarely can a phone be just dusted, as it is one of the most frequently used objects in the house. Clean it with the already-wet furniture polishing cloth. It's a mess to spray the phone directly, as there are all sorts of nooks and crannies. Only if the phone is extraordinarily dirty should you spray it directly with furniture polish, and use your toothbrush to dislodge dirt from crevices. Unravel a tangled cord by unplugging one end and uncoiling it. To avoid leaving fingerprints, polish the body of the phone first and then the handset. Likewise, replace the handset not with your bare hand but with the polishing cloth wrapped around it. (It takes time for the polish to dry on such nonporous surfaces, during which time objects fall prey to fingerprints.)

Mini-blinds

On the window are dusty miniature blinds. Lower them to their full length and turn the slats to the closed position so the blinds curve *away* from you. By grasping the string that runs through them, pull them away from the window so you can reach behind them with your feather duster. Dust them using long *downward only* strokes at a slow speed so the feather duster can do more dust-catching than dust-storming. Remember, stop the feather duster dead still at the end of each stroke. Now turn the slats forward so the blind curves *toward* you. Dust the front in the same long, slow *downward* motions.

The Family Room

This room is often full and well used. This makes it doubly important that you follow the Speed Cleaning method exactly.

The TV, the VCR, and the Stereo

The TV is cleaned by using a feather duster on the back and blue juice on the body and screen. Use your feather duster on the VCR. To remove fingerprints, spray red juice on your cloth and wipe them off. Make sure you don't get red (or any other kind of) juice anywhere near videotapes or the inner machinery of the VCR. Also use your feather duster on the stereo, being careful not to snag the tone arm or needle and thereby destroy the cartridge you just paid a day's salary for. Use your already damp furniture polish cloth to remove fingerprints from the plastic dust cover or spray it directly if it's very dusty to protect against scratches in the soft plastic.

YOU'RE FINISHED!

It's not quite time for your nap yet—but it's getting close. All that remains is the vacuuming!

Things Often Overlooked by Distracted Dusters

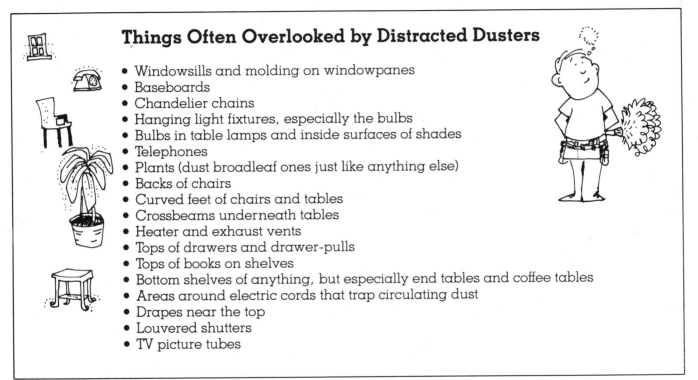

- Windowsills and molding on windowpanes
- Baseboards
- Chandelier chains
- Hanging light fixtures, especially the bulbs
- Bulbs in table lamps and inside surfaces of shades
- Telephones
- Plants (dust broadleaf ones just like anything else)
- Backs of chairs
- Curved feet of chairs and tables
- Crossbeams underneath tables
- Heater and exhaust vents
- Tops of drawers and drawer-pulls
- Tops of books on shelves
- Bottom shelves of anything, but especially end tables and coffee tables
- Areas around electric cords that trap circulating dust
- Drapes near the top
- Louvered shutters
- TV picture tubes

VACUUMING

There Are Two of Them

In a fair world you are part of a team and therefore need two vacuums, since the opportunity to save even more time justifies the expense. In an unfair world you have to get by with one vacuum. Let's assume it's fair for now and ignore the accumulating evidence to the contrary.

Their Uses

Use the bigger, canister vacuum ("Big Vac") on carpets and rugs. Use the smaller, portable vacuum ("Little Vac") on hardwood floors, the kitchen floor, and upholstery.

How to Vacuum with the Big Vac

The most important point in vacuuming is to follow Rule 1. Therefore, you plug the vacuum in once and then vacuum the entire house without

ever replugging it. This little idea saves you 20 percent or more vacuuming time right there. You never backtrack (sound familiar?) to first unplug and then go looking for another plug in the next room—which is often behind the TV or couch or in some other infuriating spot.

To accomplish this feat we use a 50-foot extension cord. Fifty feet should do it unless your home is very large. The cord is stored on a cord caddy that keeps it from tangling and tying itself into knots.

The ideal outlet is also as close to your starting point as possible while still allowing you to vacuum the entire house without replugging. This also means that most of the cord will be *behind* you as you vacuum, which is faster than working toward the cord. Take the time to keep the cord behind you and untangled.

Take the vacuum and extension cord (on its caddy) to your starting point (see sketch). Unwrap the vacuum cord and connect it to the extension cord only after tying them together in a simple knot. This is important because it will keep them from pulling apart the first time you give the cord a little tug. Next, unwrap most of the extension cord in a neat circular pile that won't turn into a giant knot later. Unwrap and lay the last section of cord in a straight line to the electrical outlet you selected. The cord in front of you is in a straight line and is much easier to maneuver out of your way, since you can move it from side to side a few inches with the beater head of the vacuum without bending to pick it up.

The above applies to wall-to-wall carpeting without modification. If you have any exposed hardwood flooring, put the extension-cord pile on the

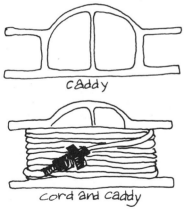

caddy

cord and caddy

hardwood floor nearest to where you will start vacuuming the rug. Otherwise you'd have to pick the pile up to start vacuuming.

Floors

Start vacuuming in the room where the Duster started, and work toward the right. Vacuum systematically, so you don't overlook an area or do it more than once. Usually you can do a living room in three fairly equal parts. Use furniture in the room as landmarks to divide up the room so you don't overlap or skip areas. Vacuum with one hand, keeping the other hand available to move furniture or other items out of your way.

Typical vacuuming is a forward and backward motion. Go forward one full length of the vacuum hose each time. Move sideways one full width of the vacuum head with each backward motion. Keep the canister part of the vacuum to your left as you vacuum the room to your right. Be very careful as you pull the canister, because if an accident can happen it will. (If you're using an upright vacuum, move forward one long step and then backward one and a half steps, because your backward steps are shorter.)

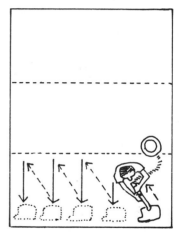

If some areas to be vacuumed are well traveled and need extra attention, then vacuum more slowly, or repeat each push and pull of the vacuum. If an area is little used, then speed up and don't go over it twice.

Furniture

The Duster has left you signals to save time. An overlapped cushion tells you to vacuum the tops of the cushions only. Just move your beater-bar

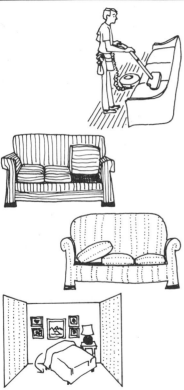

from the floor to the cushion and vacuum away. This will not harm most fabrics. But don't use the beater on very loose-fitting fabric and be careful of tassels or loose strings. (Use the Little Vac instead.) A turned-up cushion tells you to vacuum the entire couch. You use the Little Vac to do this, so leave the upturned cushion alone since that will be done later. If your vacuum doesn't have a motorized beater head don't use it to vacuum cushions or furniture. In other words, don't use a nonmotorized floor attachment, because it will transfer all sorts of fuzz from the floor to the furniture.

The signal to vacuum under a piece of furniture is when it is moved out at an angle from its normal position. Put the furniture back in its original position afterward.

Moving the Furniture

The rule is to move the item as short a distance as possible: Tip a chair back, for example, instead of transporting it. If you're helping someone by moving furniture as someone else vacuums, lift the furniture straight up, let your partner vacuum the area, and then replace it. If you're vacuuming on your own, you will have learned not to leave trays, mops, the Little Vac, trash, etc., in your direct path. Move one end of a table an inch or two to vacuum where the legs were, and then replace.

Usually it's a good idea for you *not* to replace chairs and other displaced furniture. Better to carry on vacuuming and let someone else (or you) replace items at the end of cleaning. Vacuuming is often the longest job and every step possible should be taken to avoid stopping once you've started. For example, when you reach a spot where the vacuum head doesn't fit and an act of Congress is required to get it to fit—like moving a heavy plant, or a desk, etc.—then this area should already have been cleaned with a whisk broom, feather duster, or dust cloth.

Stairs

Start at the top and vacuum your way down. If you have a canister vacuum, set it six or eight stairs down from the top. Then move it down six or eight more when you vacuum down to it. Carry a whisk broom in your back pocket to clean out corners of the stairs as needed. If you have pets, you will probably need to whisk each step before vacuuming. It's easy and fast. Whisk several steps and then vacuum several steps and repeat. Vacuum with back-and-forth motions of the beater head—not side to side. Do be careful as you vacuum backward down the stairs because we don't want to lose you.

Throw Rugs

Stand on one end of the throw rug to keep it in place. Don't use back-and-forth motions. Always vacuum away from where you're standing, lift up the beater head at the end of a stroke, and start again to the right. (Move forward on a long rug and repeat the process, if necessary, until you reach the other end.) Then come back to the starting point, where you had been standing originally, and do that area from the other direction—

again pushing away from you and lifting the vacuum head at the end of a push.

When finished, wrap the cord around the vacuum and the extension cord around the cord caddy.

How to Vacuum with the Little Vac

Unless the Little Vac gets a lot of use (hardwood floors, for example), use it without a 50-foot extension cord. The Little Vac has several attachments. The attachment you choose depends on whether it's being used to vacuum the kitchen floor, the hardwood floors, or furniture.

When vacuuming noncarpeted floors, point the vacuum exhaust away from the area you have yet to vacuum so you don't stir up dust. Also, pay special attention to areas where there are electrical cords on the floor. The cords trap a lot of dust and debris, so slow down and vacuum carefully.

When vacuuming furniture, follow The Clean Team Rules: Start on the left side at the top and work your way down and to the right.

THE OVEN

How often you do this chore depends on how often you use the oven. It's a messy and overnight job.

The first thing to notice when contemplating cleaning the oven is whether it is a self-cleaning species. If it is, follow the manufacturer's directions, not ours, and be thankful.

As long as your oven interior is a smooth baked-enamel finish (95 percent chance), you will find this chore yucky but manageable. If you have an oven whose interior feels like fine sandpaper, you have a problem, since the oven cleaner is very difficult to remove after the cleaning process. Give up.

Spray your oven the night before you are going to clean it. You'll need the oven cleaner and the rubber gloves. Before spraying the oven, remove the racks, placing them on top of the stove *the same way you took them out* (so you don't waste time later trying to figure out which is the top and how they go back in). Also remove anything else that should be removed, such as heating coils that pull out or unplug. If your whole interior oven comes apart for removal and cleaning, leave it together and clean it our way instead.

Put old clean cloths, paper towels, or newspapers on the floor to catch any drips and overspray. Spray the interior of the oven and the door as well. Often, the racks don't need cleaning. Skip them whenever you can, as they are difficult and time-consuming. If you are *not* cleaning them, leave them on top of the stove until you are done with the oven. If you are cleaning the racks, replace them after you have sprayed the inside of the oven and *then* spray them too. Spray the oven thoroughly: A little too much is better than not enough. If you overdo it, however, oven cleaner drips out onto the floor and makes even more of a mess. Avoid the interior light and thermostat when spraying. Be sure to spray the door but not the door edges.

If you are going to clean the broiler too (wow!), then spray it now also. Just spray the broiler tray itself. Don't spray the holder grooves or underneath the broiler. Those areas don't have the cooked-on stuff and can be cleaned with red juice and your green pad. (Faster and eminently less messy.)

Put the racks back in if you haven't already, close the door, put away the oven cleaner, and go to bed. Don't heat the oven. Sweet dreams, for tomorrow you will pay!

Next day—if you are also doing the weekly cleaning of the kitchen—clean the oven before you start the regular cleaning sequence. *Don't heat the oven.* Set the trash can by the stove for now, and place a roll of paper towels or old, disposable rags (ones that are no longer good enough to use as regular cleaning cloths) next to it. Also, take your putty knife from your apron and put it on the cloths in front of the stove. You'll be using it repeatedly, and your gloves will be covered with oven cleaner. This way you'll keep the oven cleaner off your apron.

Start by *putting on the gloves!* First clean the inside of the oven door with your green pad. Use your razor on the glass door. Wipe the oven cleaner from the door. Then spray the same area with red juice and wipe it clean and dry. Clean the racks next, starting with the highest one. Use the green pad. Pull it out into the locked position to make cleaning easier. As you finish a rack, pull it out and set it in the sink. Rinse it well with tap water. Be careful not to scratch the sink. (Use a cloth or two to put under the edges of the rack when rinsing.) After all the oven cleaner is removed, just let the racks drain and dry in the sink while you return to clean the next one down. As you clean them, pay special attention to the leading edges (the ones that you see when the rack is in the oven).

After the racks, clean the inside of the oven starting with the inside top. Systematically agitate with your green pad over the entire top of the oven until all the baked-on residue is loose. But don't remove it yet. Move on to the right side, then the rear, and then the left side before you finish with the bottom. On areas where there are baked on "lumps" (usually the bottom only) use your scraper first (remember, it's on the floor in front of the oven). The idea is to knock off most of what you're removing with the scraper first and then get what little remains with the green pad. Saves a lot of time.

Here the concept of "seeing through" the mess of what you're cleaning has particular meaning. Even if the oven were clean, you couldn't see through the oven cleaner. And unless you're much more compulsive than

cleaning

we are, your oven is not clean. You can quickly learn the difference between how your green pad feels when the oven surface is clean and how it feels on a dirty surface that needs additional scrubbing.

This "see-through" process is also especially important here because removing the oven cleaner is a big chore. If you've missed crud and have to respray and reclean, you may be tempted to give up cooking rather than go through it again.

Even after you've used your putty knife to remove lumps, be prepared to quickly grab for it again when you encounter something that your green pad doesn't easily remove.

As you have well noticed, your green pad became a slimy, gooey, even yucky mess about half a second after you started this delightful chore. Resist the impulse to go to the sink and rinse the pad out. It will return to a slimy mess half a second after you return. It actually works just as well dirty for a long time. And of course, the whole procedure is much faster if you don't make several trips to the sink to rinse.

When the pad is full of gunk and oven cleaner it is harder to hold because it gets slippery. Try to overcome this by folding the pad in half or gripping it differently or squeezing it out onto the oven bottom—anything to avoid having to rinse it. When you just can't grip it any longer, go rinse it. Also if the oven is very dirty (especially when you're cleaning the bottom), your pad will lose its effectiveness when it gets thoroughly clogged with debris. When that happens, it's also time to go rinse. (Sounds like something your dentist would say.)

After you have gone over the entire oven this way, rinse out the green scratch pad and scraper and put them in your apron. Start wiping the inside of the oven using paper towels or old rags. Wipe it out just the reverse of the way you just scrubbed it. Start with the bottom, then the left side, the rear, the right side, and finally the top. Wipe the entire oven out once, rather thoroughly—discarding the towels or rags into the trash can next to you. Now spray the entire inside of the oven with red juice and wipe clean and dry to get rid of any residual oven cleaner.

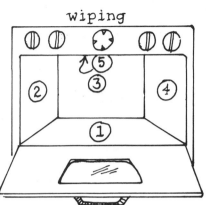

wiping

If the broiler was previously sprayed, now is the time to finish it. (Don't you really want to do this some other day?) Clean it in the sink with your green pad. Use your scraper if necessary . . . and it usually is. Protect the sink by putting cloths under the broiler. Rinse it clean, wipe it, and replace it.

Fold up the cloths (or paper towels), pick up the newspapers and discard into the trash, take a deep breath, and start cleaning the kitchen. It's a good idea to turn the oven on to 400° for 15 minutes while you start cleaning the kitchen. This cooks any oven cleaner you may have missed to a nice visible white powder that you can easily see to remove after the oven cools off. Also, if the oven is going to stink or smoke a bit, it's a good idea to get that little episode over with now instead of when you have company over for dinner.

You have cleaned an oven! Amazing how much better it looks—and you get all the credit! You may be tempted to go outside and stop strangers to bring them in and show them your clean oven. Resist: They may track in dirt.

THE REFRIGERATOR

This is not weekly cleaning. However, if you are going to clean the refrigerator when you do your regular cleaning of the kitchen, do it first—before anything else. If the freezer is to be cleaned, it should have been turned off earlier so that it is defrosted and ready to clean. You can help yourself further with this chore by choosing a time to clean it when it's as empty of food as it gets (according to your weekly shopping schedule). Also, before starting, throw out anything that deserves it.

The freezer is easy to clean once the ice is loose. Put any loose ice and ice-cube trays in the sink and proceed to clean. If possible, don't remove anything else. Rather, move items toward the right, spray the left with red juice, and wipe. Now move items from the right to the left and repeat. You may have to do that in three moves or more. If the freezer is completely full, remove only as much as you have to. When you move items to make room for cleaning, move them onto the top shelf of the refrigerator.

Inside the refrigerator itself, start with the top shelf. These interior shelves don't usually need to be emptied. Items on the shelves should not be removed—just moved to the right. Then clean the racks with red juice and white pad, followed by a cleaning cloth to wipe dry. If the shelves are too full to move things to the side, then remove only enough so you can move the rest from side to side. When you remove items from a shelf, set them on the floor just in front of the refrigerator in the order they were removed. After cleaning, replace the items in reverse order.

Do the next lower shelf and the next until you are finished. Drawers and bins should be removed from the refrigerator because you need to clean them inside and out. Don't forget that nasty area under the bottom drawers. A lot of crud accumulates here as well as some water.

Generally you can clean the door shelves by removing a few items, cleaning that space, and then sliding over a few more things and cleaning under them, etc. Be sure to wipe the bottom of these items as you put them back to where they were, so they won't leave a spot on the clean surface.

When you are finished with the inside of the refrigerator, don't clean the outside yet. Go back and start to clean the kitchen as you normally would. If you are working as part of a team, it often makes sense to have another team member do the inside of the refrigerator as you begin to clean the rest of the kitchen. The reason is that the kitchen can be the longest job, and you want the team to all finish at the same time. (See Chapter 9.)

TEAM CLEANING

Goal

You may be lucky enough to have one or two others to work with. If so, someone needs to delegate the tasks and have a good overall view of the work as it progresses. That person is the Team Leader. The primary responsibility of the Team Leader is to see that all team members finish cleaning at the exact same time.

Finally, Some Decisions to Make

To finish together requires some decision making on your part. Like, where do you start cleaning so you'll finish together? When the Bathroom Person finishes his/her primary job, what's next? The same for the Kitchen Person.

The Longest Job

The key to finishing together is to identify the longest job and get it started at the right time. The longest job is the one that takes the longest time *and* that no one can help with. This is often the vacuuming.

When this longest job should be started is crucial. Get the longest job started so it isn't still going on when the rest of the team is finished.

The graph on p. 110 shows time wasted by starting the longest job (vacuuming) at the wrong time.

However, in this same example, if the Duster had dusted only 10 minutes, started the vacuuming, and then finished dusting, the whole team would have finished together. (See p. 111). They also would finish the entire housecleaning 18 minutes faster apiece—that's nearly one full hour less total cleaning time!

The First Time

The first time you clean your home you should start dusting in the living room. If you later find you're unable to avoid having the team end up in the same room toward the end of the cleaning job, then change your starting point to the master bedroom.

When the Other Team Members Finish Their First Job

As Team Leader, you should ask *whoever* finished first (usually the Bathroom Person) to start vacuuming in the rooms you have already dusted. He or she should start where you did and follow your same path.

When the Kitchen Person finishes, have him or her make the beds with you (assuming you make beds when you clean). *Don't* make a bed alone since two people can make a bed four times faster than one person. Then have the Kitchen Person start vacuuming the hardwood floors (using the Little Vac), also starting in the living room and following your same path through the house. The Kitchen Person can also use the Little Vac on any furniture as signaled by you. Next, he or she gathers up the trash by going from room to room and emptying smaller containers into the largest one so only one trip outside to the garbage can is made.

Important Points: Back to Basics

We hope all this doesn't sound difficult, because doing it is very easy:

1. If the longest job isn't finished when the rest of the jobs are, then start the longest job sooner the next time you clean.

2. If you all end up in the same room at the end, then dust that room sooner or vacuum it sooner or empty the trash from it sooner.

3. If the dusting job is taking too long, then have a second team member do some of the dusting.

4. If you aren't finishing together even after getting the longest job started earlier, save all the short jobs for last—emptying trash, making bed(s), putting throw rugs back in place, finishing touches, and checking each other's work (nicely, nicely).

5. If you still have problems finishing together, sit down and talk about it. Don't feel that just because you're Team Leader you are alone in a boat adrift. Try suggestions that come from the other team members.

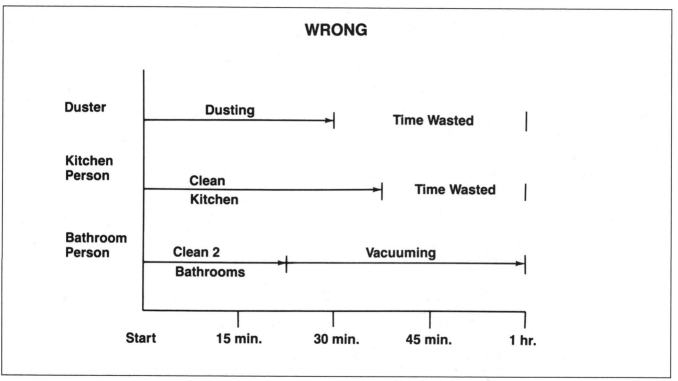

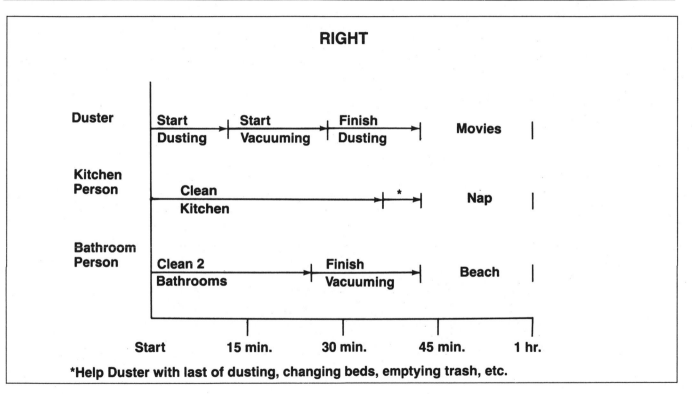

RIGHT

Duster — Start Dusting | Start Vacuuming | Finish Dusting — Movies

Kitchen Person — Clean Kitchen — * — Nap

Bathroom Person — Clean 2 Bathrooms | Finish Vacuuming — Beach

Start | 15 min. | 30 min. | 45 min. | 1 hr.

*Help Duster with last of dusting, changing beds, emptying trash, etc.

Team Cleaning in a Team of Three or More

Most of what we've discussed in this manual applies to a team of three. The jobs are a Kitchen Person, a Bathroom Person, and the Duster. Teams of four or more are so inefficient that you may want to rotate people off each time you clean.

Team Cleaning in a Team of Two

In a team of two, one person starts as the Bathroom Person and the other as the Kitchen Person. The Team Leader is the one who finishes the initial assignment first—normally the bathroom. The Team Leader then changes the bathroom tray into a duster tray and starts dusting. The Kitchen Person starts vacuuming with the Big Vac after finishing the kitchen. Make adjustments so that each time the two of you clean you come closer and closer to finishing at the same time. It is much simpler for two people to finish at the same time than three, since there are fewer possibilities for how to divide up the work.

Team Cleaning in a Team of One

This is the most efficient way possible. No decisions, no negotiations—just follow the Speed Cleaning method and you get faster every time you do it.

Recording Your Improvement

We've provided a place for you to record your weekly housecleaning times so you can see how dramatically your time improves (see the Appendix, p. 119). Be sure to use it to keep up the interest of the other members of your team during this critical learning period. It would also be a good idea to remove it from this manual and post it where it is easily seen, reviewed, and ultimately admired.

AN ENCOURAGING WORD

Warning

Don't read this chapter until after you've used "the method" on your home the first time. Okay? Okay.

The Honest Truth

Now that you've cleaned the house using our Speed Cleaning method, what do you have to say?

"My red and blue juice fell out of the apron hooks every time I turned a corner or even breathed!"

"Geez, you wouldn't believe how awful it was. My red and blue juice fell out of their apron hook every time I turned or bent over!"

"The stupid top came off my spray bottle twice. I spent more time cleaning up those messes than I would have to clean my own way."

"It takes so long to get the bottles back into their apron loops it would be faster to set them down on the floor or somewhere and pick them up again."

"It's too much to remember—what to do when and what tool to use."

"There's no way I'll get any faster. It feels awkward and funny."

"I like my old way better. It was even faster."

Did we miss any? Oh yes, how about:

"I did it your way, except I didn't use the apron since it doesn't really help me that much."

Now that you have the complaints off your chest, do you feel better? Good.

Let's talk.

The Other Honest Truth

Did you ever despair of learning to tie your shoe, ride a bike, or swim? Can you remember how difficult it was to do something that is now mindless in its simplicity?

Did you ever learn touch-typing? If you did, you know that it took you longer to use touch-typing than your old hunt-and-peck method when you were first learning. You had to break comfortable old (inefficient) habits and replace them with unfamiliar, uncomfortable, and new (but very efficient) habits.

Also, if you used your old hunt-and-peck method of typing all day long every day, you would never, ever get much faster than 30 words a minute—even with all that practice. However, if you practiced your new touch-type method daily you would improve your speed constantly: 100 words per minute is not an unheard-of speed. That's more than three times faster than a method that once seemed just fine to you.

Housecleaning isn't going to go away, so practice. Practice and be fast, and then do something much more fun with all the time you saved.

OTHER TYPES OF CLEANING

More!?

For those of you who see all the time-savings available in the preceding chapters but feel that your particular cleaning problem is still ignored and still overwhelming, you may be right.

Cleaning Categories

There are three types of household cleaning. One is weekly cleaning, which is the subject of this book. Unfortunately, there is also daily cleaning (clutter) and yearly spring cleaning. Clearly, you are going to have trouble with the weekly cleaning if no one is doing the daily cleaning.

Daily Cleaning (Clutter)

Daily cleaning is putting things in their place—day in and day out. Dirty dishes from the table (or TV room) into the dishwasher. Coats on their hangers. Dirty clothes into the hamper. The trash set out. The toys put away.

There are those who complain about "clutter" because they throw things any old place and are then faced with the "uncluttering" job of picking them up and returning them to where they belong. Of course, it takes *less* time to "throw" things where they correctly belong and *never even be faced with the problem*. However, you already knew that.

Best Solution

The best solution for reducing clutter is to handle each item once so it never gets a chance to become clutter. Put it away. Takes about 2 seconds. Try it. If that doesn't work you have too much stuff. Add a room, buy more furniture, or have a garage sale.

2nd Best Solution

It may help to have designated "clutter areas." Once you have designated clutter areas it's okay to throw things into them. Examples may be the corner next to the front door, one section of the kitchen counter, or the bedroom floor near the closet. After you get in the habit of putting things

away in these areas, slowly reduce their size and then finally eliminate them.

Also, as promised in the introduction, once you start regular cleaning, these daily jobs will take care of themselves as a sense of pride in a clean home encourages everyone in the household to keep the home civilized between cleanings.

Yearly Cleaning (Spring Cleaning)

This is cleaning out the cupboards and closets and drawers. Washing walls. Or washing (heaven forbid) the windows. All those things that only need your cleaning attention once or twice a year. But that's another story.

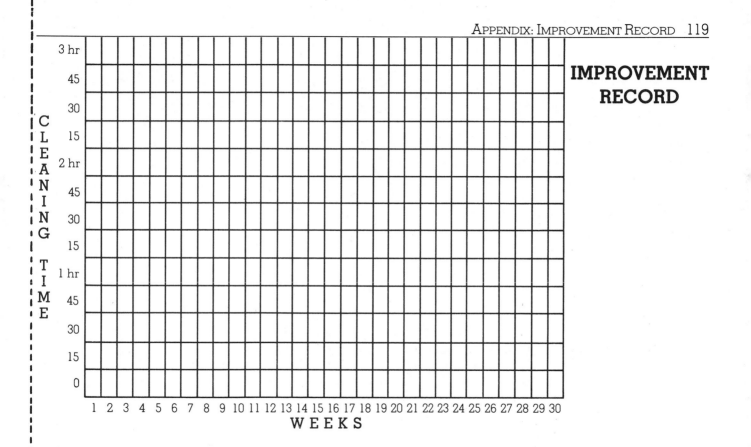

IMPROVEMENT RECORD